1979 And The Re-Emergence Of The Islamic Empire

A Monograph
by
Major Thomas M. Hough
United States Army

School of Advanced Military Studies
United States Army Command and General Staff College
Fort Leavenworth, Kansas

AY 2009

SCHOOL OF ADVANCED MILITARY STUDIES

MONOGRAPH APPROVAL

MAJOR Thomas M. Hough

1979 And The Re-Emergence Of The Islamic Empire

Approved by:

_____   Monograph Director
Alice A. Butler-Smith, Ph.D.

_____   Director,
Stefan Banach, COL, IN   School of Advanced
                                        Military Studies

_____   Director,
Robert F. Baumann, Ph.D.   Graduate Degree
                                        Programs

Abstract

1979 and the re-emergence of the Islamic Empire by Major Thomas M. Hough, U.S. Army, 59 pages.

In 1979 the age old struggle for the control of Islam between the Shiite and Sunni sects re-emerged in the Middle East. Four events occurred in 1979 that defined the context of contemporary Middle Eastern politics: the Islamic revolution in Iran, the signing of the Egyptian-Israeli peace accords, the siege of the Grand Mosque in Mecca, Saudi Arabia, and the Soviet invasion of Afghanistan. This monograph directly addresses the roots of current Middle Eastern actors such as HAMAS, FATA, Hezbollah, Al-Qaida, and the Taliban in the aftermath of these four critical events that occurred in 1979.

The methodology for this monograph consists of analyzing each of these four events and then synthesizing this information in order to determine how 1979 shaped the modern Middle East. Since the seventeenth century the Sunni sect dominated Islam. The Iranian revolution re-energized the Shiite sect throughout the Middle East while Sunni power simultaneously eroded throughout the region. While the Shiites were inspiring the Islamic community in 1979, the Sunni suffered significant blows to their legitimacy as the leaders of Islam.

This monograph asserts that the prevailing conflict within the Middle East is first and foremost a contest between the Shiites and the Sunni for preeminence within the Islamic world. The conflict between Islam and the outside world remains secondary in importance. The contemporary Middle Eastern actors that dominate the western consciousness such as HAMMAS, FATA, Hezbollah, Al-Qaida, and the Taliban constitute proxy armies created by the Shiite and Sunni leadership to wage a war for influence within the Islamic world. The events of 1979 have resulted in a leveling of power in the Middle East and the emergence of the Shiites as an ideological peer competitor to the traditionally dominant Sunni.

TABLE OF CONTENTS

1979 And The Re-emergence Of The Islamic Empire

Deep understanding of one's own culture is challenging – it is even more difficult to analyze others. However, for the United States and in particular the United States military and civilians in Iraq and Afghanistan, it is essential to understand the dynamics of the Middle East. With thousands of years of recorded history dating back to the time of the Persian invasions of Greece and complicated by sixteen-hundred years of Islamic history starting with the prophet Mohammed in the seventh century, trying to figure out where to start can be intimidating.[1] However, one year in the past half century stands alone, and that year is 1979.

Four significant events occurred in 1979 that have had the effect of reinvigorating an empire and changing the dynamic of the Middle East from one characterized by Sunni domination to one shaped by Sunni and Shiite competition. These four events are the Islamic revolution in Iran, the Egyptian—Israeli peace treaty, the assault on the Grand Mosque by Islamic extremists in Saudi Arabia, and finally the Soviet invasion of Afghanistan. These four events had the effect of once again elevating Islam to the center stage of politics in the Middle East region.

Since the independence movement of the 1930s, the newly independent Sunni nation states of Egypt, Saudi Arabia, Jordan, Syria, and Iraq struggled with transition from an Islamic Caliphate to the western nation state system. Prior to this, the people of the region had primarily been divided between those under the Sunni Ottoman Empire and those under the Shiite Sufavids Empire providing governance for its subjects, with Islam as both the religion and the state.[2] However, since the independence movement following World War I, the Middle East had followed a western model of governance, one heavily influenced by the British, French, and other

---

[1] Stephen Tanner, *Afghanistan: A Military History from Alexander the Great to the Fall of the Taliban* (Cambridge: Perseus Book Group, 2002), 10-11.

[2] Ambassador Ryan Crocker, "Lessons of Diplomacy in the Middle East" (lecture, Command and General Staff College, Ft. Leavenworth, KS, April 23, 2009).

western powers.[3] By 1979, the Middle Eastern people believed that Pan-Arabism, secularism, and traditional monarchies had all failed the Islamic World.

Under the nation state model, secular governments rose to power in the Islamic world. Islam was no longer understood to be the unifying characteristic of the people. Nationalism, ethnocentrism, and political affiliation took the leading role in defining identities. The Sunni Arabs unified against a common foe, Israel. However, after thirty years of Sunni led assaults against Israel between 1948 and 1978, the Jewish nation not only still existed, but had grown stronger and, in many ways, exhausted its Sunni adversaries. A rivalry for control of the Sunni brand of Islam persisted between the Egyptian powers marketing Arabism and Saudi Arabia promoting Islamism. Both nations stood to gain from their efforts, as Egypt was the historic birthplace of the Arabs, and Saudi Arabia was the birthplace of Islam. In 1979, this debate was decided when Egypt signed the Egypt—Israel Peace Treaty. For Egypt this move was necessary to realign the country with the United States, a move that deterred the Soviet plan to bring Egypt into the USSR sphere of influence. The peace treaty was the cost of doing business with the United States. The upside for Egypt was access to western economic and military power. The down side was a clear break between Egypt and the rest of the Arab world. The path was now clear for Saudi Arabia to ascend above Egypt as the strongest power in the Islamic world. While the leaders of Saudi Arabia were anticipating external challenges to the kingdom for expansion of their influence over the Sunni, a violent threat emerged from within. In November, 1979 the Grand Mosque in Mecca, the holiest shrine in all of Islam, was taken by force by Islamic extremists. This event exposed the weakness of the royal family of Saudi Arabia, Al-Saud, and quickly put Saudi Arabia on the defensive, a position in which the kingdom still finds itself.

---

[3] Howard M. Sachar, *The Emergence of the Middle East: 1914-1924* (New York: Alfred A Knopf, 1969), 252-290.

More importantly it left the Islamic world adrift without clear leadership, something that Ayatollah Khomeini and his Shiite Islamic revolution in Iran planned to exploit.

With Egypt ending the unity of the Arab League in March with the Egyptian-Israeli Peace Treaty, Saudi Arabia experiencing a major domestic crisis in the November assault on the Grand Mosque, and Iran in the midst of a revolution, the Soviet Union invaded Afghanistan in December, 1979. Over the next thirty years this event created the second of two fronts in the war for Islam. On the eastern front of the traditional Islamic empire are the Sunni. After defeating the Soviet superpower as part of the U.S. coalition during the Soviet-Afghan war, the Saudis attempted to remake the east in its own image - a plan that has backfired and produced organizations such as Al-Qaeda, who now threaten Saudi Arabia and its western allies. On the western front is the Levant region consisting of Lebanon, Israel, and the Sinai Peninsula. A region abandoned by the Sunni and adopted by the Shiites in their effort to gain control over Islam. In this region the Shiites have also defeated a superpower, the United States, and through their proxy armies, Hezbollah and Hamas, won a strategic propaganda war against Israel. Something the Sunnis failed to do during their thirty years of war with Israel. The result of these four events in 1979 is that the historic struggle for Islam between Shiite and Sunni has been revived. Pan-Islamism has re-emerged as the dominant ideology of the Middle East and the western model of governance based upon the treaty of Westphalia is under assault. The west is a part of the war for the control of Islam. However, this war is not about the west: it is about Sunnis and Shiites competing to decide the future of the Middle East. 1979 is the year this struggle re-emerged.

Iran: 1979 A Shiite Empire is Re-born

Iran: Transformation from Persia to the Land of the Aryans

The conditions that brought about the Islamic revolution in 1979 were rooted in 1921. In that year, Reza Khan began a military coup that resulted in his ascendance to the Peacock Throne in 1923. Reza Khan became Reza Shah Pahlavi and replaced the last of the Qajars dynasty in 1923 as the new shah of Iran.[4] Reza Shah desired change to the old Persian status quo system in which power belonged to land owners who had little incentive to modernize the nation, and move it towards independence from its landowner elites and western influencers. The Shah has been described by Kenneth Pollack, author of *The Persian Puzzle*, as "[o]bsessed with modernity and industrialization; committed to secularization; devoutly nationalist; enamored of a powerful, modern military; ruthless and dictatorial in his methods; and determined to create a new Iranian man."[5] During this time period, the Shah pursued the western nation state model, much like his Sunni neighbors.

Reza Shah envisioned an Iran restored to its rightful place as a Middle Eastern empire, modeled on its pre-Islamic Persian history.[6] To accomplish this task the Shah attempted to break the nation's ties with Shiite Islam, the agrarian based economic system, and the tribal social system. During his tenure he relied upon his military skills to build a force capable of bringing the various factions of Iran together under a central government in Tehran.[7] Also, Reza Shah began to insist that foreigners call the nation Iran and not Persia, reflecting the fact that the nation consisted of many ethnicities.[8] Due to the Soviet Union's refusal to leave Iran post World War II,

---

[4] Kenneth M. Pollack, *The Persian Puzzle* (New York: Random House, 2004), 27.

[5] Ibid., 28.

[6] Yapp, *The Near East Since the First World War* (New York: Longman Group , 1991), 174.

[7] Pollack, 31.

[8] Ibid, 31.

a strong military was essential for Reza Shah to minimize foreign intervention that posed a destabilizing threat to his new regime. With the country stabilized and a military prepared to defend the borders of the nation, Reza Shah embarked upon a monumental modernization program that drastically changed the landscape of Iran. According to author Kenneth Pollack, from 1925 to 1942, Reza-lead initiatives resulted in "…14,000 miles of roads, 6,000 miles of telephone lines, he abolished Shari'a courts, guaranteed religious minorities equal protection under the law, and modernized the status of women."[9] By embracing the industrial revolution and even post-industrial issues such as women's suffrage and religious freedoms, Reza Shah was preparing Iran to compete with Western powers. Beliefs of Reza Shah are best described by Iranian expert and author Ray Takeyh who said, "[m]ore than any other nation, Iran has always perceived itself as the natural hegemon of its neighborhood."[10]

Most of Iran's neighbors, especially to the west, had been dramatically affected by World War I owing to fall of the Ottoman Empire. Iran, although mainly unscathed by the events of World War I, became a necessary component of the Allied strategy in World War II. The railroads built under the leadership of Reza Shah that stretched from the Persian Gulf to the Caspian Sea were needed by the Allies to resupply the Russian Army on the eastern front with Germany. Reza Shah denied the British and Russian request to utilize the rail system, and for this the foreigners exiled him from the country after an embarrassing two-week military campaign after which his forces folded to the allies. As stated by Pollack, "[o]n August 25, 1941, his twenty-one year old son, Mohammad Reza Shah Pahlavi replaced his father on the Peacock Throne in Tehran."[11]

---

[9] Ibid, 34.

[10] Ray Takeyh, *Hidden Iran: Paradox and Power in the Islamic Republic* (New York: Henry Holt and Company, 2006), 61.

[11] Pollack, 38.

The reign of Shah Mohammad Reza from 1942 to 1979 was defined by three significant events. The Shah wanted to maintain autonomy from both the U.S. and USSR sphere of influence. The Prime Minister Mossadegh was overthrown by the United States. And finally, the Shah initiated reforms known as the White Revolution to increase his popularity with the people, however, these reforms failed.

The Shah struggled to maintain autonomy from the U.S. and USSR. After the occupation of Iran by British, U.S. and Russian forces during World War II, the Allied powers agreed upon a simultaneous withdraw by spring 1946.[12] The Russians, however, saw the opportunity to annex part, or all, of Iran into the new Soviet empire by enticing various minority populations such as the Kurds, Azeris, and a growing communist party to overthrow the Shah and install a regime favorable to the Soviets. For this reason, the Soviets refused to withdraw their forces in 1946. Pollack's statement, "Iran thus had the honor of becoming the arena for the first crisis of the Cold War, and it fell to the United States to solve the problem," demonstrates the importance of Iran.[13] The Truman administration triumphed and eventually brought about a Soviet capitulation, identifying Iran as a nation of national security interest for the United States. The United States attempted to build Iranian capacity to modernize its economy and oil industry and serve as a U.S. surrogate against communism in the Middle East. The rise to power of Mohammad Mosaddeq would complicate the effort and change the fate of U.S. and Iranian relations.

The United States and its western allies perceived Mohammad Mosaddeq as irrational. The west also believed that Mosaddeq promoted "…an extreme form of Iranian nationalism."[14] Mosaddeq presented two problems for the west. First, he did not allow any concessions for the British in the ongoing oil dispute between the two nations. Mosaddeq fulfilled his campaign

---

[12] Ibid. 44.

[13] Ibid. 45.

[14] Ibid. 59.

promises to the Iranian people by kicking the British Anglo-Iranian Oil Company out of Iran and taking over the British oil refinery at Abadan on the Persian Gulf.[15] In 1951, the British asked President Truman for assistance in overthrowing the Mosaddeq, President Truman refused.

In 1952 Mosaddeq was involved with the rigging of Iranian elections to protect his base of power with the nation's communist party. Over the next year his behavior became more radical and unpredictable leading President Eisenhower to believe that Mosaddeq – quoted by Pollack, "…could not be reasoned with when he took office in 1953."[16] Mosaddeq continued to taunt the United States believing that, as stated by Pollack, "…the United States considered Iran a vital nation, and that Washington would never risk losing Iran to the Communists."[17] The threat of the USSR gaining a foothold in Iran was enough to prompt the Eisenhower administration to interfere in Iranian internal political issues. U. S. Central Intelligence Agency arranged for the overthrow of Mosaddeq in August 1953, thus securing the reign of Mohammad Reza Shah. While this may seem an insignificant event in history, author Stephen Kinzer states, "…in Iran almost everyone has for decades known that the United States was responsible for putting an end to democratic rule in 1953 and installing what became the long dictatorship of Mohammad Reza Shah. His dictatorship produced the Islamic revolution of 1979."[18] In an interview with Seyed Safavi of the Iranian Revolutionary Guard Corps in October 2007, author Robert Baer quoted Safavi as saying, "…The Mosaddeq coup was a grievous injury to American-Iranian relations, a wound as fresh as it had been four decades earlier."[19]

---

[15] Stephen Kinzer, *All The Shah's Men: An American Coup and the Roots of Middle East Terror* (Hoboken: John Wiley & Sons, 2003), 2.

[16] Pollack, 63.

[17] Ibid. 64.

[18] Kinzer, X.

[19] Robert Baer, *The Devil We Know: Dealing with the New Iranian Superpower* (New York: Random House, 2008), 240.

The final event that would set the stage for the end of the Shah's regime and the arrival of Ayatollah Khomeini was the White Revolution beginning in 1963. Mohammand Reza Shah desired the adoration of the people of Iran. After returning to the throne in 1953, the Shah devised ways to improve his popularity. He quickly determined that land reform was a popular movement and that he could capitalize on the desire of the peasantry to move out of poverty and into the landowner class. In January 1963, the Shah supported a referendum known as "…the Revolution of the Shah and the People" also known as the White Revolution.[20] The goals set out in the reform consisted of land reform, development of public lands, profit sharing, privatization of state industries, revised electoral laws to better represent blue collar workers, and a literacy program for rural residents.[21]

The revolution focused on land reform and industrial modernization. The Shah, like his father, wanted a modern Iran that could compete with the superpowers of the world and emerge as a leader in the region. The Shah used the country's ever-growing oil revenues from the mid 1960s to the mid 1970s to build an industrial base and housing for rural workers moving to the urban core. In the 1960s approximately one-third of the Iranian population lived in towns, by 1979 that number would be over half.[22] The population increased dramatically owing to the better access to health care in the cities. The government subsidized many of the industries, which enabled worker compensation; however, even with the tremendous increase in oil prices and revenue for the government, many people's lives did not improve.

The heart of the populist movement, land reform, did not turn out as planned. While many peasants did get a land grant from the government, the rich landowners were able to hold onto the most valuable property. Over time the majority of peasants ended up selling their small

---

[20] Pollack, 86.

[21] Ibid.

[22] Yapp, *The Near East Since the First World War*, 330.

parcels back to the original landowners and moving to the cities, creating more of a burden on the nation's economy.[23] By choosing the peasantry over the landowners the Shah, stated by Pollack, "...deprived himself of that power base and alienated the one class most committed to the monarchy."[24] The White Revolution turned into a disappointment for the nation's poor who by the mid 1970s found their lives no better and in many cases worse than when the revolution began in 1963. The land owning class had returned to its original power position in the country, however, they were no longer supporters of the Shah who had attempted to take their land from them. The only ally the Shah had left by the 1970s was the Americans.

For Ayatollah Khomeini, the situation in Iran was playing to his strengths and his particular view of Islam. For Khomeini, according to author Ray Takeyh, "Islam has provided government for about 1,500 years. Islam has a political agenda and provides for the administration of a country."[25] Khomeini, expelled by the Shah in 1964, was still able to get his message to Iran via taped sermons sent from his home in Najaf, Iraq.[26] Khomeini capitalized upon the failures of the White Revolution and the Shah's close association with the west. Khomeini made the case that the Shah was a western proxy serving the will of the United States. Khomeini also claimed that the Shah's failure to elevate Islam was the cause of Iranian suffering.

The election of President Jimmy Carter and his inauguration in January 1977 made the situation worse. President Carter ran on a platform of human rights and foreign policy initiatives steeped in liberalism. The Iranian people expected the Carter administration to rebuke the Shah and isolate the Shah from his American support base - the Carter administration did the opposite. President Carter visited Tehran in January 1978 where he made public statements that were,

---

[23] Pollack, 91.

[24] Ibid. 87.

[25] Takeyh, 13.

[26] Pollack, 94.

according to Pollack, "…effusive in their praise of the shah," including a famous toast at the state dinner in which Carter called Iran "…an island of stability in a turbulent corner of the world."[27] What followed were massive sentiments of anti-Americanism from the Iranian population. Daily protests and riots began in early 1978. The Shiite tradition of mourning the dead for forty days created a cyclical pattern of protests, death, and violent memorial services.[28] This violent pattern culminated in the revolution that ended the Shah's tenure and began the reign of Ayatollah Khomeini.

The Death of Persia: The 1979 Islamic Revolution

Many have documented the actual events of the 1979 Islamic revolution in Iran. Less understood is the purpose of the revolution and its impact on the Middle East and greater Muslim world. Clearly many at the time of the revolution, especially in the west, believed the words and goals of Ayatollah Khomeini were rhetoric used to motivate the religious base in Iran. What is more clear today in retrospect, is that Khomeini's words were more than rhetoric and that thirty years of revolutionary transformation has produced an Iran modeled on his ideas. To understand the Iran of today, it is essential to understand the goals of the revolution, how the revolution affected the Middle East, and the effect of the revolution on the other significant events of 1979. To understand the revolution, you must understand Khomeini.

At a macro level, five themes define the ideology of Ayatollah Ruhollah Khomeini. Those five themes are politics, religion, authoritarian power, xenophobia, and nationalism. Khomeini had a distinct advantage over his peer religious scholars in Iran during the 1960s and 1970s. Due to his expulsion from Iran in 1964 Khomeini traveled to Turkey and finally settled in

---

[27] Ibid, 124.

[28] Ibid. 129.

Najaf, Iraq, the home of Iraq's great Shiite leaders.[29] This exposed Khomeini to the rest of the Middle East where he was able to experience the sweeping Pan-Islamist movement during the 1970s that was promoted by Saudi Arabia.[30] Khomeini understood the ebbing tide of support for the secular Pan-Arab movement after the defeat of the Arab Armies in 1967 by Israel. He understood that the religious class in the Middle East was under assault by secular regimes and that Shiites in particular were being suppressed by Sunni elites. In Najaf, Khomeini not only preached his ideology for his Iranian audience, he also targeted the greater Shiite audience. This strategy paid off in the long term as the majority of the future leaders of Hezbollah were students of Khomeini at the Shiite seminary in Najaf, Iraq.[31]

Khomeini was not popular and did not agree with most of his clerical peers that religion should avoid politics. Khomeini viewed politics as clearly in the preview of the clerics and a vehicle to spread his ideology. Author Ray Takeyh stated, "[f]ar more than his clerical brethren, Khomeini proved to be a man of his time, and he sensed that the changing politics of Iran offered a unique opportunity to propagate his Islamic ideology."[32] Khomeini demonstrated his political savvy throughout the revolution. When students first overran the American Embassy on February 14, 1979 Khomeini denounced the attacks and ensured the repatriation of the Americans. When students overran the Embassy again on November 4, 1979, Khomeini supported the attack.[33] Khomeini understood the need for popular support and the importance of timing in the political arena. The taking of the embassy supported his goals. However, in February, Khomeini had only been back in Iran for a few weeks and still had various powerful factions inside the country he

---

[29] Ibid. 94.

[30] Sherifa Zuhur, "Saudi Arabia: Islamic Threat, Political Reform, and the Global War on Terror" (monograph, Carlisle, Strategic Studies Institute, 2005) 20.

[31] Judith P. Harik, *Hezbollah: The Changing Face of Terrorism* (New York : I.B. Tauris, 2007), 16.

[32] Takeyh, 13.

[33] Pollack, 153.

needed to win over to his cause. A move against the Americans initially would have been too dramatic and perceived as irrational. By November, his conquest of the Iranian political landscape was complete, and the Embassy attack and the holding of American hostages fit his greater agenda of elevating Iran to the global stage.

Khomeini's embrace of politics came from his desire to revitalize religion. Takeyh states, "[f]or Islam to remain vital, he argued, it had to embrace a distinct political content and be part of the larger struggle sweeping the developing world."[34] Khomeini tailored his religious arguments to the mass base of urban poor, peasant farmers, and left wing Marxists in Iran. Khomeini displaced his religious rivals in Iran by denouncing their actions as supporting the Shah. Like any good politician, Khomeini tied the identity of his rivals to the unpopular regime in power and promised a better life to the people through religion. Khomeini was able to generate a followership who believed, just as he did, that if Iran embraced Islam, Allah would raise Iran to its rightful place as an Empire. Author Ray Takeyh noted that Khomeini preached "[d]irect assumption of political power by the clergy. After all, he observed, the Prophet of Islam was not just a spiritual guide but an administrator, and executor of justice, and a political leader."[35]

Khomeini was able to sell his concept that the future of Iran demanded Iran's embrace of Islamic jurisprudence by exploiting a "…national narrative that always mistrusted foreign elements."[36] Aware of Iran's recent history with the west, and the fresh wounds of the Mossaddeq affair in 1953, Khomeini convinced the population that their poor lot in life was because of American imperialism and the corrupt Iranian leaders, like the Shah who exploited the people for his own personal gain. Khomeini used sacred Shiite religious symbols such as the martyrdom of Hussein, and the return of the Mahdi, twelve Imam, and a historical narrative of

---

[34] Takeyh, 14

[35] Ibid. 15.

[36] Ibid. 16.

struggle against invaders to "…transform Islam into an anti-Western ideology."[37] Through this approach, Khomeini was able to attack America and its Zionist ally Israel and other regimes such as Saudi Arabia, Egypt, and other Islamic countries that cooperated with the west as well. Khomeini's vision in 1979 was more than just an Islamic theocracy in Iran; he desired to transform all of Islam into his ideological image. Khomeini not only rejected the west, he rejected the entire international relations system based on the Westphalia nation-state model. Through his re-defining of what Islam is, Khomeini was able to capture the passion of the people and transform those passions into support for his revolutionary agenda. The 1979 Iranian Islamic revolution was the re-emergence of the great Persian Empire of old, except, this time it was founded on Shiite Islam instead of Persian ethnicity. The revolution will not truly end until Iran has returned to its desired rightful place as the master of the Middle East peoples.

The energy of Khomeini's message and his dynamic leadership motivated Muslims across the region. To the dismay of House of Saud, even some Sunnis rejoiced in the fervor of Iran's revolution. In Pakistan, news of the Siege of the Grand Mosque in Mecca and the declaration by Khomeini that, as stated by Trofimov, "…it would not be far-fetched to assume that this act has been perpetrated by the criminal American imperialism so that it can infiltrate the solid ranks of Muslims by such intrigues" motivated protestors to storm the U.S. Embassy in Islamabad, Pakistan. [38] On their way home from the Haji, approximately 120 Senior Pakistani Officers went to Qom, Iran. The Officers were greeted by Khomeini who declared that the confrontation at the Grand Mosque in Saudi Arabia, the U.S. hostage crisis in Iran, as well as the attack on the U.S. embassy in Pakistan was "…not between America and Iran but between the

---

[37] Ibid. 17.

[38] Yaroslav Trofimov, *The Siege of Mecca: The 1979 uprising at Islam's Holiest Shrine* (New York: Random House, 2007), 108.

entire world of disbelief and the World of Islam."[39] Khomeini redefined the purpose of an Islamic

nation and its military. The Iranian constitution stated, "[t]he government should strive for the

political, cultural and economic unity of the Islamic world, ran the preamble; and government and

army had a duty to extend the sovereignty of God's law throughout the world."[40]

Whether intended as a grand strategy or not, the desire of Khomeini to spread his

revolution to all of Islam occurred simultaneously with his revolution in Iran. Suppressed

Muslims with any connection to Iran began to absorb the revolutionary message. Shiites in

particular looked to Iran for leadership. The 350,000 Shiites who occupy Saudi Arabia's eastern

province, home to the majority of Saudi's oil reserves, revolted against their Sunni masters.[41] The

event resulted in a weeklong standoff between Shiites and Saudi security forces, demonstrating

the effect of Iran upon its Shiite brothers throughout the Middle East.

For America, 1979 was becoming more disastrous by the month. President Carter's

National Security Advisor Zbigniew Brzezinski wrote the President, "…I am concerned over the

transformation of the conflict from Iran vs. international community into America vs. Islam."[42]

The cumulative effect of the Iranian revolution spilling over into the greater Middle East,

threatening the survival of the Al-Saud regime in Saudi Arabia and motivating attacks on U.S.

Embassies in Pakistan and Syria brought about the formulation of the Carter doctrine. The

doctrine set about an American Military build-up in the region and a "…public statement (a

'Carter Doctrine') explicitly committing U.S. military power to the defense of countries in the

region that are of vital importance to us."[43] A popular interpretation in the Middle East of the

Carter Doctrine was Sunni elites protected by American military power in exchange for access to

---

[39] Ibid. 140.

[40] Yapp, *The Near East Since the First World War*, 345.

[41] Trofimov, 179.

[42] Ibid. 218.

[43] Ibid. 219.

oil. The impact of the Khomeini Islamic revolution was to divide the Middle East between those who follow the true path of Islam led by the Iranians and those who sided with the Great Satan, the United States, and its Lesser Satan ally, Israel. At stake in 1979 was the heart of Islam. The Iranian revolution was the event that stole it away from the Sunnis and placed it in the hands of the Shiites.

Thirty Years of Revolutionary Migration: Hezbollah

1979 was a year that saw Shiite success and Sunni failures, a trend which has continued for the past thirty years. Immediately following the events of 1979, Sunnis and Shiites go head to head in the Iran-Iraq War. At the same time, the leader of the Sunnis, Saudi Arabia, and the leader of the Shiites, Iran, each fight proxy wars in the region. While they fight to a stalemate at the Shiite-Sunni border of Iraq, the Shiites emerge on the western front of the Islamic empire with an Iranian proxy Army, Hezbollah. This is the Army that defeated Israel in 2006, something the Sunnis could not do in three attempts. The Sunnis on the other hand set the conditions on the eastern front of the Islamic empire that enabled the rise of Al-Qaida, an organization that turned on the Sunnis' greatest ally, the United States, and threatens the very heart of Sunni Islam, Saudi Arabia.

On September 22, 1980, Saddam Hussein, who also rose to power in Iraq in 1979, crossed the border into Iran in an attempt to secure the oil- rich Khuzestan province.[44] Saddam was motivated not only by his greed for oil money but also by fear. Khomeini had strong ties to the Shiites of southern Iraq, because of his years spent living in Najaf, Iraq. Saddam already had security problems with the Shiite Dawa party that attempted to kill both his foreign minister and information minister in 1980.[45] Saddam believed that with the chaos of the revolution in Iran, the

---

[44] Pollack, 184.

[45] Ibid. 183.

15

invasion would be easy and possibly trigger a movement to overthrow the new regime in Tehran and replace it with something more acceptable to the Arab Sunnis. While neither side would win the conflict, the Iranians would internalize lessons learned from the conflict and turn them into best practices in their fight in Lebanon. In the battle for Khorramshahr, Iran, just across the Shatt al-Arab waterway in Iraq, the Iranians began the learning process that led to their future success. During this one battle, the Iraqis sustained, as per Pollack, "…8,000 casualties and the loss of more than 100 tanks and APCs to Iranian infantry equipped with small arms, light antitank weapons, and Molotov cocktails."[46] This idea of defeating conventional military forces through the use of unconventional means proliferated to Iran's other war for regional hegemony in Lebanon.

July 20, 1988, was the official end to the Iran-Iraq war as Ayatollah Khomeini agreed to end the conflict. During the nine-year war Iran lost hundreds of thousands of citizens, the majority of its Navy to the United States who had sided with Iraq and supported it from the Persian Gulf, and eroded Iranian public support for the Mullahs.[47] Most of this was caused by Khomeini's stubborn refusal to call an end to the conflict, even when Saddam had made various peace overtures throughout the 1980s. The lesson for Iran from the war with Iraq was that if Iran was going to fulfill its destiny to dominate Islam and the Middle East, it was going to have to do it through asymmetric means.

The Iranians opened the western front in the war to dominate the Dar-al-Islam, world of Muslim believers, in Southern Lebanon against Islam's greatest rival - Israel. A defeat of Israel by the Shiites was a means to achieving the ultimate goal of the Shiite regime in Iran, the domination of Islam. Just as the Saudis understood that a defeat of the Zionist secures their dominance and leadership over the Middle East, the Iranians understood likewise. Israel

---

[46] Ibid. 187.

[47] Ibid. 233.

presented Iran with some significant challenges. First, Israel had proven their capability in defeating Muslim Armies. Second, Iran was already at war with Iraq, blocking its lines of communication to the Levant. The Iran-Iraq War also meant that the majority of Iran's combat power was unavailable for an assault on Israel, besides the fact that an assault against a superior force was un-Islamic. Author of *War and Peace in the Law of Islam* stated, "[u]nder no circumstances, however, should the imam risk a jihad if he considers the enemy too powerful for him to win a victory, namely, if the enemy is a least twice as powerful as the Muslims."[48]

The Iranians relied upon two traditions to develop their emergent strategy against Israel. The Iranians used their Shiite credentials to gain a foothold in Southern Lebanon by relying on the role of Lebanese clerics in the transformation of Iran from Sunni to Ithna-ashari, Twelver, Shiite Islam in 1501 under the Persian Safavid dynasty.[49] At the time, Iran was a primarily Sunni dominated region with few Shiite scholars to facilitate the religious transition. "Most of their subjects being Sunnis, the Safavids called on the Arab Ulema from Jabal Amil [region of Southern Lebanon], Mesopotamia [Southern Iraq], and Bahrain to help create a clerical infrastructure, leading to the earliest instance of a 'remembered' historical connection between 'Iran' and 'Lebanon'."[50] This historical fact gave the Iranians a cultural bridge to their desired subjects, the Lebanese Shiites. The Iranians might not have a geographic border with Israel, but their Lebanese Shiite brothers did.

To solve the second problem of a lack of available resources to mount an Iranian attack on Israel, the Ayatollah relied on the Islamic concept of Dawah to get the Lebanese Shiites to

---

[48] Majid Khadduri, *War and Peace in the Law of Islam* (London: The John Hopkins Press, 1955), 67.

[49] H.E.Chehabi, ed. *Distant Relations: Iran and Lebanon in the last 500 years* (Oxford: The Centre for Lebanese Studies, 2006), 3.

50 Ibid. 4.

fight for Iran. Dawah, a concept of "…inviting people in handsome ways"[51] was used to coax the Lebanese into doing Iran's fighting against the Israelis. The desire for the Lebanese became more urgent when the Israelis entered the Lebanese Civil War on June 6, 1982, crossing Israel's Northern border into Southern Lebanon.[52] The first Iranian Revolutionary Guards arrived in Damascus, Syria on June 12, 1982 and from there moved to the Becca Valley to train Shiite forces.[53]

Over the next several years, the Iranian proxy force achieved one success after another, bombing the U.S. embassy in Beirut in April 1983 and the Marine Barracks in October. This success ushered in a campaign of terrorism against westerners, who were targeted for kidnapping and assassination by guerilla fighters. Iran achieved its first victory in the Levant on February 7, 1984, when the Regan administration and its European allies withdrew all western troops from Lebanon. This left Lebanon wide open for the Iranians and placed the most important issue in the Muslim world, the fate of the Palestinians, within the grasp of the Iranians. Khomeini had declared, "…the matter of Palestine is an Islamic issue."[54] This placed Shiite Iran in position to embrace the Sunni Palestinians who knew only rejection and neglect from their Pan-Arab leaders.

Hezbollah emerged from the success of Iran in Southern Lebanon in the early part of the 1980s. The impact of the success of the Islamic revolution, the Shiite connection, and Iranian supported social programs in the spirit of Dawah had won over the Lebanese Shiites. Hezbollah, conceptualized by a "…circle of young Lebanese mullahs" who "…identify with the Revolution's ideology and embraced the principle of government by the Supreme Jurist"[55] became Iran's Army against the Israeli occupation of Lebanon. During the 1990s, Hezbollah mastered the art of

---

51 S.K. Malik, *The Quaranic Concept of War* (Delhi: Adam Publishers, 1992), Preface.

52 Baer, 57.

53 Ibid. 52.

54 Ibid. 68.

55 Harik, 16.

guerilla warfare and provided funding and training from Iran's Revolutionary Guard Corps to anti-Israeli forces became common practice. In May 2000, Israel withdrew from Lebanon handing Hezbollah and its Iranian masters a tremendous win for the Shiites. Of the success, Ayatollah Khamenei, Khomeini's successor after his death in 1989, stated, "Lebanon is Iran's greatest foreign policy success. We will repeat it across Dar al-Islam [the Islamic world] until all of Islam is liberated."[56]

Hezbollah and Iran capitalized upon this success in 2000 by winning seats in the Lebanese parliament, essentially legitimizing Hezbollah as a political party. The dream of Khomeini that had inspired a revolution in 1979 became a partial reality by 2006; a Shiite Army had defeated Israel. The Iranians had pulled Lebanon and Syria into their sphere of influence during the process, building upon their Middle East Empire. The "…Shia crescent" defined by King Abdullah of Jordan as a Shiite arc of influence across the region had become more solidified.[57] For the Shiite, the dream conceived in 1979 is moving from the impossible to the conceivable. The Shiite control of Mecca and with it the control of Islam under a Shiite Empire is within Iran's grasp. Iranian success in Lebanon through Hezbollah is the blueprint.

Egypt in 1979; The End of Egyptian History

End of the Ottoman Empire to 1979: The Sick Old Man Became Contagious

According to Ambassador Ryan Crocker, the most significant date in Middle East foreign relations is 1798, the year Napoleon landed his Army in Egypt.[58] Britain later occupied Egypt in 1822 and retained ownership of Egypt until granting independence in 1922 with caveats that maintained British control of the Suez Canal and Egyptian defense and foreign policy. This

---

[56] Baer, 55.

[57] Ian Black, "Fear of a Shia Full Moon," *Guardian,* January 26, 2007, under "Shia Crescent," http://www.guardian.co.uk/world/2007/jan/26/worlddispatch.ianblack (accessed July 12, 2009).

[58] Ambassador Ryan Crocker, "Lessons of Diplomacy in the Middle East" (lecture, Command and General Staff College, Ft. Leavenworth, KS, April 23, 2009).

meddling of Western powers in Egyptian foreign policy gave rise to the Egyptian revolution of 1952 described as the "…first radical revolution in the Arabic-speaking countries of the Near East (Middle East)."[59] A group of military officers known as the free officers led by Lieutenant Colonel Jamal Abd al-Nasser led this revolution.[60] This group dominated Egyptian politics for the next twenty years and set the conditions for the most unlikely of all events in Egypt in 1979, peace with Israel.

Nasser reorganized the power structure of Egypt between a presidential government supported by a parliament and a single political party. Nasser and his fellow free officers filled the majority of important government billets and essentially militarized the Egyptian government. The Nasser design was to create support for his regime amongst the people through socialism. "Between 1952 and 1972 the public sector grew from 15 percent to 48 percent of gross domestic product (GDP)."[61] For Nasser, conquering Egypt and creating a system in which he was the most powerful citizen of a socialist state was only the first step. The next move for the ambitious Nasser was to become the most dominant figure in the Middle East. Nasser needed to find a common linkage to the Middle Eastern people around the Levant. Adb al-Nasser himself "[d]escribed three circles within which Egypt moved: the Islamic, African and Arab."[62] Nasser chose Arab identity as the center of gravity for an Egyptian rise to regional hegemony. His ideology, Pan-Arabism, called for all Arabs to look past their national borders towards Egypt, the cradle of Arab civilization for leadership. To gain the support of the Arab world Nasser would have to prove the worth of his Pan-Arab movement. The unifying issue for Arabs at the time was the destruction of Israel and the return of Jerusalem, a holy city for Muslims as well as Christians

---

[59] Yapp, *The Near East Since the First World War*, 211.

[60] Ibid.

[61] Ibid., 218.

[62] Ibid., 221.

and Jews, to Arab control.[63] Nasser also pushed back against the west in 1955 by agreeing to buy weapons for his expanding Army from Czechoslovakia, then a member of the USSR. In 1956 Nasser completed the Egyptian split with western powers by nationalizing the Suez Canal, creating the Suez Crisis with Britain, France, and Israel in the fall of 1956. "The events of 1955 and 1956 transformed Abd al-Nasser from an Egyptian into an Arab leader and ushered in a period of more than ten years when Egypt played a dominant role in Arab affairs as the leader of opposition to Israel, a perpetual challenge to traditional regimes and the central element in all schemes of Arab unity."[64]

By trying to dominate the Arab world, Nasser not only made enemies abroad, he also aggravated other regional power brokers such as Saudi Arabia and Jordan. Saudi Arabia believed it was the leader of the Middle East because of its championing of the Pan-Islamism ideology. The Egyptian entry into the Yemeni civil war created even more hostility as Egypt became embroiled in the geopolitics of the Arabian Peninsula, something Saudi Arabia viewed as clearly within their domain.[65] Egypt also became the primary sponsor of the Palestinian movement and the founder of the Palestinian Liberation Organization, a movement that threatened the stability of Jordan and its Hashemite royal family. The support for Yemen cost Egypt a third of its Army and approximately four billion dollars (1967 dollars), and the support for the Palestinians brought about the 1967 war with Israel. The 1967 war was a dramatic turning point for Egypt. As a consequence of the war Egypt lost the Sinai Peninsula with its oil reserves and the Suez Canal, which was a major source of revenue for Egypt. Not only was the Sinai lost—"…in six days, those three Arab states (Egypt, Syria, Jordan) lost East Jerusalem, the West Bank, the Gaza Strip,

_____

[63] David Fromkin, *A Peace To End All Peace: Creating The Modern Middle East 1914-1922* (New York: Henry Holt and Company, 1989), 313.

[64] Yapp, *The Near East Since the First World War*, 221.

[65] Ibid.

the Sinai Peninsula and the Golan Heights."[66] After the massive 1967 Arab defeat, everyone including Egyptians began to turn on Nasser and his Pan-Arab movement, making room for the Islamic fundamentalism that had been brewing in Egypt since the founding of the Muslim Brotherhood by Hasan al-Banna in 1928.[67]

The Muslim Brotherhood movement, as stated by Schanzer, "[e]nvisioned the return to a time marked by a global Islamist order [the caliphate] in which Islam reigned supreme through one devout Muslim ruler [the caliph]."[68] The Muslim Brotherhood was the only real domestic threat to Nasser's regime during his rise to power. Nasser was able to counteract the fundamentalist movement by offering the people a competing ideology, Pan-Arabism, and by brutal suppression of the Muslim Brotherhood. Nasser in his desire to socialize Egypt, brought the public and a vast majority of the private education system under government control. The regime also outlawed the Sharia courts that had been responsible for civil disputes. In 1965 the government executed Sayyid Qutb, the ideological leader of the Muslim Brotherhood and writer whose books *Milestones* and *Signposts* remain two of the most influential documents in the Islamic fundamentalists' movement to this day.[69] The combination of Nasser's suppression of Islam and his decision to execute the Muslim Brotherhood's spokesperson combined with the Arab defeat of 1967 left Egypt uncertain of its future by the early 1970s. M.E. Yapp stated, "[Nasser] died on 28 September 1970 before any clear lines for the future development of Egypt had been established and with no decision on the choice of a pathway out of her foreign policy dilemmas."[70]

---

[66] Jonathan Schanzer, *HAMAS Vs. FATAH: The Struggle For Palestine.* (New York: Palgrave MacMillan, 2008), 18.

[67] Albert Hourani, *A History of the Arab Peoples.* (New York: Warner Books Edition, 1991), 348.

[68] Schanzer, 13.

[69] Daniel Benjamin and Steven Simon, *The Age Of Sacred Terror* (New York: Random House, 2002), 62.

[70] Yapp, 223.

Vice-president Anwar al-Sadat assumed the presidency from Nasser.[71] Sadat recognized that Egypt was adrift with no strategic guidance from the leadership. Without immediate success, the growing fundamentalist threat from the Muslim Brotherhood enflamed by the regional support of Pan-Islamism from Saudi Arabia would become the future of Egypt. Sadat found himself the leader of a nation that prided itself as the cultural birthplace of Arabs, and the most historically significant place of all humanity. The reality in 1970, however, was that Egypt was nearly bankrupt, its Army had not recovered from Israel's surprise attack in 1962 and the country was slowly becoming the vassal of the Soviet Union. Sadat believed that his first move must be to restore the pride of Egypt and that of the Arab peoples before the country could move forward. He did not believe that Egypt had any hope of negotiating from a position of weakness with Israel, Saudi Arabia, or the Soviet Union who all had plans for what Egypt's role in the region should become.[72]

In 1973, Sadat executed a counter-offensive against the Israeli position on the Suez Canal. While militarily the operation was a draw, fighting with the Israelis allowed Sadat to claim victory and gain the trust of the Egyptian people, which he needed to begin charting a new path for Egypt. Sadat now had the political capital to begin the process of reform he envisioned for Egypt - a process of liberal democratization - something alien within the Middle East.

Throughout the 1970s Sadat engineered sweeping social changes in Egypt, from the establishment of a multi-party political system to the freeing of foreign trade and investment.[73] Sadat's strategy was to defeat the Islamists within Egypt and prevent the country from being drawn even deeper into the Soviet sphere of influence. He planned to do this by providing a better life for the people. This new vision for Egypt rested on Western democratic principles. By

---

[71] Ibid.

[72] David W. Lesch, *1979: The Year That Shaped the Modern Middle East* (Cambridge: Westview Press, 2001), 35.

[73] Yapp, 226.

doing so, Sadat began to create space for Egypt and the United States to develop a partnership. Sadat needed U.S. economic assistance and political support to push back against the USSR, and the U.S. needed an ally in the region to broach the Israeli peace process. In 1976, Sadat cancelled a treaty with the USSR, as well as Soviet rights to use Egyptian bases.[74] Sadat was not ready to turn the future of Egypt over to yet another western power which had an interest in using Egypt as a regional proxy. Peace negotiations between Israel and the Arabs began with the Geneva conference with both U.S. and USSR support. Sadat high-jacked the process in 1977 with a surprise visit to Jerusalem. It was the first such visit of an Arab leader to Israel since its inception in 1948. This set the precedent for direct negotiations between Israel and Egypt and set the stage for the most dramatic non-violent critical event of 1979, the Egyptian-Israeli peace treaty.

1979 Egyptian recognition of Israel: The Death of the Arabs

On March 26, 1979, Anwar al-Sadat stunned the world by signing the Egyptian - Israel treaty recognizing the state of Israel. In return, the Israelis agreed to vacate the Sinai Peninsula. For Sadat's actions Egypt's Arab neighbors and Muslim cohorts ostracized and expelled Egypt from the Arab League.[75] Moreover, the Middle Eastern community took it upon themselves to publically criticize the actions of Egypt. For Ayatollah Khomeini it was important to point out that this crime against Islamic law came at the hands of an Arab Sunni. Khomeini now ranking Egypt in the same category as other smaller Satans, as stated by Takeyh, "…He [Khomeini] derisively condemned the Gulf states, Egypt, Saudi Arabia, and other American allies as mini-Satans who served to accommodate the transgressions of the "Great Satan."[76]

---

[74] Ibid., 228.

[75] Ibid., 229.

[76] Takeyh, 19.

The 1979 peace deal had the effect of moving the politics of the Middle East between two opposite ends of the spectrum – fundamentally Islamic or fundamentally western. This left political moderates between these two positions. With Egypt moving in one direction and Saudi Arabia moving in another, unity as Arabs was no longer possible.

On one side was Egypt which had clearly come into the U.S. sphere of influence. Although initially rejected by its Arab neighbors, Egypt believed that over time and through economic success, and its historical narrative as the birthplace of Arabs, Egypt could convince some of its former allies to move forward in recognizing Israel.[77] Since 1979 Egypt has depended on the willingness of the United States to stay engaged in the Middle East and pursue the peace process for the Levant.

On the other end of the spectrum in 1979 is Iran. Although no clear causal relationship exists between the Egyptian - Israeli peace treaty and the Islamic revolution in Iran, the fact that they occur simultaneously creates an atmosphere of dichotomy in the Middle East. To side with Egypt is to recognize Israel and the imperial nature of U.S. involvement in Islamic affairs. To side with Iran is to recognize that, as stated by Khomeini in 1979, "…the matter of Palestine is an Islamic issue."[78] Iran placed itself in a position as the clear leader of the Islamic movement, openly supporting the destruction of Israel and curtailment of U.S. influence in the region.

In 1979 the political moderates were the al-Saud royal family of Saudi Arabia, the Hashemites of Jordan, Syria and the Saddam Hussein regime in Iraq. While these regimes had participated in the 1948, 1967, and 1973 campaigns to defeat Israel, they had done so with Egypt as a clear partner and more importantly as the second front against the state of Israel. With Egypt at peace, this front was gone. These nations could either follow suit and make peace with Israel on their own terms or take up the Islamic challenge of Khomeini. For the Saudis, the Iranian

---

[77] Yapp, *The Near East Since the First World War*, 229.

[78] Baer, 68.

Islamic revolution challenged their mantle of Pan-Islamic leadership. However, Saudi Arabia could not afford to be as openly hostile towards the United States and its ally Israel owing to its close economic ties with the west. This left the Sunni Saudis and the Sunni Hashemites in a position of weakness, hemorrhaging from both the far left and right of the Middle Eastern population. The dilution of Egyptian Pan-Arab leadership left Iraq as a free radical on the front lines between the weakening Sunni power and growing Shiite entity, creating opportunity for exploitation - an opportunity upon which Saddam would capitalize with the invasion of Iran in 1980.

While unquestionably the least violent of all the significant events in the Middle East in 1979, the Egyptian destruction of Pan-Arab unity and movement into the western ideological camp had a tremendous impact. For the region it meant that the Sunni dominance as a force against Israel had been superseded by Shiite leadership. The Shiites were in a position to unify opposition to the occupation of Islamic holy ground by the Zionists. For the Egyptian Muslim Brotherhood it meant that the fight for an Islamic state of Egypt was postponed indefinitely. The Muslim Brotherhood, which had been an organization against the use of violence to achieve its goals since its founding in 1928, would begin to transform. From the Muslim Brotherhood emerged numerous Islamic fundamentalist groups and individuals to include Ayman Zawahiri who left Egypt for Saudi Arabia, attracted by the Sunni Islamic movement underway in the kingdom.[79] The same Zawahiri would later become the right hand man for Osama Bin Laden and his Al-Qaeda movement that is currently leading the Sunni Islamic war for control of the Middle East. Also from the 1979 events in Egypt emerged Hamas and Fatah. Although both are Sunni organizations, over the next thirty years in the war between Shiite and Sunni they have become instrumental indicators of the nature of the conflict, and most importantly, who's winning.

---

[79] Trofimov, 43.

The Power of Shiite Dawa: How Shiite Iran won over Sunni Hamas

The issue of Palestine and the recognition of Israel by Egypt split the Muslim Brotherhood. Schanzer stated,"[t]he younger, more zealous Islamists believed that Israel had to be conquered (and become Palestine)" while "…the old guard, which represented the longstanding Brotherhood approach, held that nonviolent outreach [dawa] was the way to slowly retake Palestine."[80] This divide was a motivation for the founding of Palestinian Islamic Jihad (PIJ) in 1979. This group, founded by two Gaza based Islamists, "…sought to leverage the momentum of Ayatollah Ruhollah Khomeini's Iranian revolution of that year."[81] The group became part of a much larger movement of Islamism within Egypt. Through this movement the group found the members it needed to pull off its ultimate act of defiance, the assassination of Sadat. A member of the Egyptian military, Khalid Islambouli, assassinated the leader of Egypt during a parade commemorating the 1973 Egyptian victory over Israel on October 6, 1981.[82]

The assassination of Sadat brought about a severe crackdown on Islamist movements under the new President of Egypt, Hosni Mubarak. To escape persecution and possible death by torture at the hands of the Egyptian military, many members of the Muslim Brotherhood escaped to Saudi Arabia and Palestine.[83] Inspired by Khomeini's calls for the destruction of Israel and their own success killing the "Pharaoh" of Egypt, the PIJ looked to transform the Palestinian movement.[84] PIJ had become the leader of the Palestinian Islamic movement by the time of the 1987-1988 intifada (uprising). Owing to their overwhelming success targeting Israeli Defense Forces (IDF) the PIJ became the target of a major Israeli operation to decimate the group. The IDF was successful at targeting the PIJ, as stated by Schanzer, "…thus, the stage was set for yet

---

[80] Schanzer, 21.

[81] Ibid.

[82] Benjamin and Simon, 83.

[83] Harik, 12.

[84] Benjamin and Simon, 83.

another splinter organization of the Muslim Brotherhood to explode onto the Palestinian political scene."[85] This new group was Hamas: They would become the major Palestinian challenger to Israel and to Yasser Arafat's Fatah-backed Palestinian Liberation Organization (PLO).

Arafat founded Fatah in 1958 in Kuwait. The purpose of Fatah was to overthrow Israel, and "…raise a Palestinian flag over the land that had been conquered by Israel."[86] Fatah commenced attack on Israel from its base in the West Bank and earned the respect of the Palestinian people for their efforts. With the defeat of the Arab allies by Israel in 1967 the Arab leadership was looking for a new leader in the fight for Arab Palestinians. In Yasser Arafat they found a charismatic leader who could continue the Arab fight against Israel while allowing the Arab governments some degree of deniability and creating some political space for them to distance themselves from the violence. In 1974, "[t]he PLO was recognized as the unquestionable leader of the Palestinian people at an Arab summit" and Yasser Arafat was recognized as the "…sole legitimate representative of the Palestinian people."[87] Under his leadership Fatah continued to serve as an inner political elite, a base of trusted advisors around which he would build the greater Palestinian Liberation Organization structure.

At the same time that Arafat and the PLO organization were consolidating their position, a rival group was growing in the Gaza Strip. This rising power, popularity, and violent nature of the PLO caught the Israelis off guard. Israeli leaders quickly determined that the counter to the PLO was the Muslim Brotherhood organization which in its past had denounced violence against Israel and support only dawa, non-violent, means of dissent. As a counterweight to the PLO the Israeli military "…provided Ahmed Yassin, the eventual founder of Hamas, with a license to

---

[85] Schanzer, 22.

[86] Ibid., 17.

[87] Ibid., 19.

establish al-Mujamma' al-Islami - the Islamic Center.[88] For the next 15 years, his center served as a political and cultural center for most Brotherhood activities in the Gaza Strip."[89] The infrastructure of his network became the foundation of Hamas and by 1988 the organization was competing with the Fatah-led PLO for control of Palestine.

The ideological difference between the Fatah-led PLO and Hamas reflects the 1979 death of Pan-Arabism and the emergence of a regional Islamist movement inspired by Saudi Arabia and now led by Iran. Yasser Arafat retained the old Pan-Arab ways of defining success as the destruction of Israel and the establishment of Palestine in its place, with him as the new President. Over time his organization faced many of the same corruption allegations and scandals that many of the other Arab regimes in the region were experiencing. Hamas had a larger vision grounded in the modern Islamic movement inspired by the events of 1979. Matthew Levitt stated, "[w]hile the immediate goal of replacing Israel with an Islamist Palestinian state is Hamas' overarching priority, the group also sees itself as leading a broader, pan-Islamist international movement."[90] Yasser Arafat and his Fatah party essentially failed to understand, or capitalize upon, the growing Islamic movement in the region and attempted to play the same political games pursued by the Arab League. Just as Sunni Islam suffered continuous fracturing and setbacks since 1979, the Fatah led PLO has followed suit, losing its base of support in the Gaza Strip and slowly seceding to Hamas.

As the Shiite Iranian presence in the Levant grew from 1979 onward, the ability of Iran to influence the Arab Sunni Palestinians has also grown. The 1979 Khomeini-inspired Islamic Jihad organization by the mid 1990s, as stated by Levitt, "[b]egan training at Hezbollah camps in Lebanon, under the supervision of Iranian Revolutionary Guards stationed in the country, and

---

[88] Ibid., 20.

[89] Ibid.

[90] Matthew Levitt, *HAMAS: Politics, Charity, and Terrorism in the Service of Jihad* (New Haven: Yale University Press, 2006), 9.

carried out some joint operations with Hezbollah camps in Lebanon."[91] By 1993, both Hamas and Islamic Jihad joined the Damascus-based Alliance of Palestinian Forces and "…set aside their differences."[92] The Alliance of Palestinian Forces, with headquarters in Damascus, Syria is a front organization controlled by Iran to coordinate activities of other groups with Iran's proxy army, Hezbollah.[93]

Over time Iran has become the leader in the fight against Israel. With every victory against Israel the Shiites widen the gap between the Muslim Middle East and the Sunni Arab leaders. The Iranians understand the dynamic change in the region since 1979 and that the Islamic movement for the masses is not quintessentially Shiite or Sunni, but Islamic. For this reason, Iran has been able to coax Sunni Arab organizations such as Hamas and Islamic Jihad, whose roots lie in the traditions of the Muslim Brotherhood, and bring them under their wing.

Saudi Arabia and 1979; A Royal Families Fight for Survival
From the Death of the Sick Old Man to the Birth of a New Islamic Kingdom

To understand the significance of the 1979 crisis in Saudi Arabia, it is important to first understand what Saudi Arabia is. Saudi Arabia is a family. The history of Saudi Arabia from 1932 to the crisis of 1979 is a history of promoting the royal family and ensuring their survival against their enemies. As the birthplace of Islam and the home of the two holiest sites in the entire Muslim world, Mecca and Medina, Saudi Arabia has assumed the role as leader of the Islamic faithful. In the mind of the royal family - the Al-Saud's - no other nation, individual, or organization have a legitimate claim to the mantle of leadership of the Muslim population. Survival of the royal family and their dominance over power in Saudi Arabia as well as the Saudi

---

[91] Ibid., 26.

[92] Ibid.

[93] Ibid.

hubris towards their role as the only leaders of Islam, explain the actions of Saudi Arabia from its inception in 1932 until the 1979 crisis.

Abdelaziz al-Saud began his conquest for Arabia in January 1902. Abdelaziz followed the example of his ancestors who were companions of Ibn Abdel Wahhab, founder of Wahhabism. Abdelaziz organized Wahhabi warriors and terrorized Arabia during the Ottoman Empire. In a surprise attack of now legendary scale, Abdel Aziz organized a small band of Ikhwan warriors who killed the governor of Riyadh and spread Wahhabism across the Nejd region of Arabia.[94] For the next fifteen years, Abdel Aziz used the Ikhwan warriors to spread control by the sword across the Arabian Peninsula. By the 1920s, the future king had attracted many followers and begun to establish a legitimate Army for the protection of his domain. The Ikhwan Bedouin warriors became a problem as they raided into British controlled territories along the northern border of Arabia. According to M.E. Yapp, "[b]y the late 1920s the Ikhwan were an embarrassment which threatened both internal security and foreign intervention because of the animosity aroused in neighboring states by their raids." [95] In March 1929 Abdel Aziz' troops put down the Ikhwan in a final battle as Abdel Aziz moved the region towards statehood.[96] Arabia became independent in 1932 as the Kingdom of Saudi Arabia, named after King Abdel Aziz al-Saud. The basis for governance was that "…all administration is in the hands of his Majesty King Abd al-Aziz ibn Saud. His majesty is bound by the laws of the Sharia."[97] Thus, Abdel Aziz al-Saud had made a deal. The various factions and tribes permitted Aziz al-Saud to rule the Hijaz and Najd region as a unified kingdom as long as Sharia law was the only law of the

---

[94] Trofimov, 16.

[95] Yapp, *The Near East Since the First World War*, 191.

[96] Trofimov, 16.

[97] Yapp, *The Near East Since the First World War*, 189.

land. This created a strong conservative base for the King, a base founded on the teaching of Ibn Abdel Wahhab and his Wahhabi followers.

The event that would begin to separate the royal family from its Wahhabi base was the discovery of oil and the recognition of Saudi Arabia's vast oil reserves by the west. Although Standard Oil was exporting oil from Saudi Arabia by 1938, substantial oil exporting did not begin until 1944, the year the Arabian American Oil Company (ARAMCO) began to run the Saudi oil industry.[98] The recognition of Saudi Arabia's economic importance by the world's newest post World War II superpower, the United States, occurred in 1945 when King Abdel Aziz met with U.S. President Roosevelt on the deck of an American warship in Egypt's Great Bitter Lake.[99] With the vast infusion of oil wealth that would occur over the next thirty years, the monarchy had the resources to transition Saudi Arabia away from a loosely federated kingdom of tribes immersed in Wahhabi values to a modern Westphalian nation state that could dominate the Middle East region.

King Abdel Aziz died in 1953 and the throne passed to his son King Faisal.[100] The transition from father to son was a precarious time for the Al-Saud family. Yaroslav Trofimov describes the period as a time where "[f]ellow monarchies on Saudi Arabia's doorstep collapsed one after another in bloody revolutions, swept away by the nationalists fervor that followed the Arab armies' humiliating defeat by the nascent Israeli state in Palestine."[101] Power had changed hands in Iraq, Egypt, and Yemen during this time period and the effect on the new king was to reinforce the idea that Saudi Arabian governance must be designed to protect the survival of the royal family above all else.

---

[98] Ibid., 192.

[99] Trofimov, 19.

[100] Ibid., 20.

[101] Ibid., 21.

King Faisal's view was that the security of the royal family resided in exploiting the family's role as the leadership and protectorate of Islam. Saudi Arabia's peer competitor at the time, Egypt, under the leadership of Nasser, promoted secular Arab nationalism as the social glue for the Middle East. This ideology was a direct challenge to Saudi Arabia since Egypt was the accepted historical birthplace of the Arabs. Faisal recognized that the protection of the royal family could occur through the growth of Saudi influence in the region and that Islam was the key to the family's influence. Pan-Islamism, the idea that a person's defining identity is Islam, worked for King Faisal on two fronts. First, it legitimized the idea of the Al-Saud family as the rightful representatives of Islam in their role as monarch of the Islamic holy land. Secondly, by promoting Sunni Islam the King could appease the royal family's Wahhabi base that was essential to protecting the royal family from enemies internal to Saudi Arabia.

To promote his Pan-Islamic movement, King Faisal developed an ingenious plan to reintroduce Saudi Arabia's influence on Islam. King Faisal would invest millions of dollars in the one place that all Muslims must travel to during their lifetimes, the Grand Mosque in Mecca. To complete the transformation of the modest mosque into a forty-five acre wonder, King Faisal employed his trusted friend Mohammed Bin Laden, the father of Osama Bin Laden, as the contractor to complete the enormous work.[102]

King Faisal would also reach out to Egypt's Islamic fundamentalist group, the Muslim Brotherhood, as they were expelled by the secular Nasser regime. "As part of his Pan-Islamic outreach, King Faisal also invited into the kingdom thousands of members of the Muslim Brotherhood, the secretive fundamentalists organization that preached the destruction of secular Arab regimes."[103] One of the Egyptian immigrants to Saudi Arabia was Mohammed Qutb, the brother of Sayyid Qutb, the revered author of *Milestones*, and an iconic symbol of the Islamic

---

[102] Ibid.

[103] Ibid., 22.

fundamentalist movement. Mohammed Qutb and many of the other Muslim Brotherhood members worked in Saudi Arabia as teachers. One of their pupils was Osama Bin Laden. [104]

A growing movement for modernization and human rights was also challenging the Kingdom. An imported worker population, primarily ARAMCO employees who accounted for one third of the nation's population of six million, promoted this movement. [105] Although the Kingdom attempted to keep these foreigners separated from the Saudi population, the transfer of western ideology and culture occurred. To appease his western allies who financed and ran the Kingdom's oil industry, the King made concessions. King Faisal outlawed slavery, promoted education for women and introduced Saudi television. [106] The King's initiatives sparked protests from the far right conservatives on the religious spectrum. However, his growing popularity from the success of the Pan-Islamists movement following the defeat of the Pan-Arab leaders in the 1967 Arab-Israeli war left little room for criticism by Saudi Arabia's most conservative citizens. [107] Saudi Arabia's agreement to fund Syrian and Egyptian militaries, both non-oil bearing countries, to re-attack Israel in 1973 - this time successfully - continued to build upon Faisal's popularity and the success of his Pan-Islamist movement.

Not everyone on the home front was happy with the rapid changes occurring under the King Faisal regime. The Saudi government was able to afford the latest technologies and rapidly built housing complexes around its cities for the Saudi Arabian people. Rapid modernization and urbanization had the effect of moving the traditional conservative tribal peoples such as the Ikhwan away from traditional homelands and lifestyles. For the Bedouins who had recently moved to the city, this was foreign, unwanted, and an un-Islamic way for the House of Saud to

---

[104] Ibid.

[105] Ibid., 23.

[106] Ibid., 22.

[107] Ibid., 23.

treat people. The rift that had started between the Wahhabi traditionalists and the royal family shortly after the discovery of oil became further exacerbated. The introduction of Salafi fundamentalism imported from Egypt's Muslim Brotherhood into the Wahhabi society would be the foundation for a growing Islamic extremist movement. The Kingdom's weak domestic security institutions misinterpreted this movement as support for King Faisal's Pan-Islamism or simple venting of frustrations by the Kingdom's conservative Wahhabi.

The royal family's insulation from the population made it difficult to recognize the threat they had created with a disgruntled Wahhabi population under the influence of Salafi fundamentalists. The Al-Saud family became preoccupied with the popularity of the regime and the success of the Pan-Islamist movement. This popularity in the Middle East brought the royal family what they desired the most, protection of their status quo position as sole rulers of Saudi Arabia. The revenues from oil since the 1973 oil embargo continued to climb each year allowing the royal family to increase their standard of living.[108] The popularity of the King was high and the recognition of Saudi Arabia as the leader of the Islamic world was secure. However, the assassination of King Faisal in 1975 by a nephew would consume the full attention of the royal elites for the next several years.[109] The crown passed to his brother Khaled who had little desire to serve as king.[110] Real power resided in the hands of his brother Fahd, the First Deputy Prime Minister. Games of royal intrigue reminiscent of eighteen-century Europe consumed the royal family. The Al-Saud family did not see the traumatic events of 1979 on the horizon. The Iranian Islamic revolution and other related events of that year would fundamentally surprise Saudi Arabia. The high water mark of Al-Saud influence gave way to a turning tide of Shiite dominance of the Middle East and the greater Muslim world.

---

[108] Ibid.

[109] Yapp, *The Near East Since the First World War*, 358.

[110] Trofimov, 24.

The Siege of the Grand Mosque

The sheer audacity of the Grand Mosque attackers lead by Juhayman al Uteybi and the utter surprise and incompetent response by the Saudi security forces demonstrated just how much the royal family were out of touch with their people. For the Saudi leadership, 1979 was a year of many surprises. While the regime focused on internal domestic issues, in the region "…Ayatollah Khomeini returned to Teheran on February 1, effectively signaling the end of the reign of Muhammad Reza Pahlavi, the Shah of Iran".[111] On March 26, 1979, another shock to the Saudi Monarchy occurred with the Egyptian-Israeli peace treaty signed by Israeli Prime Minister Menachem Begin and Egyptian President Anwar Sadat at the U.S. White House.[112]

Saudi Arabia had envisioned itself as the regional hegemony of the Middle East and leader of the Muslim faithful. These two events would begin to crack the identity that Saudi Arabia had of itself and reduce Saudi influence in the region. Egypt had made peace with the Jewish state that Saudi Arabia used as a source of antipathy to build upon their Islamic leadership credentials. Saudi Arabia had even funded Egypt's and Syria's 1973 victory against Israel, a war that had restored a level of pride to the Arab street and attributed to the leadership of the Saudi Kingdom. The actions of Sadat deflated the idea of a Saudi sphere of influence over all Sunni Muslims.

The Iranian Islamic revolution would work in tandem with the Egyptian-Israeli peace treaty to demystify the influence of Saudi Arabia. While Egypt was demonstrating that it could operate outside the influence of Saudi Arabia, Ayatollah Khomeini would challenge the Al-Saud family's Islamic credentials. As the Iranian revolution escalated throughout the summer months to a crescendo on November 4, 1979 with the taking of sixty-six American hostages at the embassy, the crack that had begun in February was now fully developed and the vulnerability of

---

[111] Lesch, 27.

[112] Ibid., 34.

the Saudi regime was exposed.[113] The seizure of the most holy site in all of Islam by fundamentalists on November 20, 1979, brought the Al-Saud regime to the breaking point.[114]

Juhayman al Uteybi and several hundred followers killed the few security guards and took over the Grand Mosque at dawn of the First of Muharram.[115] While various scholars have disputed the connection between the motivations of Juhayman and the other two significant events that occurred thus far in 1979, what is not disputed is that the Uteybi tribesman from the Nejd region of Saudi Arabia was primarily motivated by disgust with the Al-Saud leadership. Juhayman wrote, "[y]ou should know that a ruler and leader of Muslims should satisfy three conditions: be a Muslim, be a member of [Prophet Mohammed's tribe of] al Quraysh and be a man who applies the religion.[116] The Al-Saud family was not of the Quraysh tribe and according to Juhayman, did not apply the religion. Juhayman's main issues with the leadership of the Al-Saud's were the presence of westerners in the land of Allah, the close ties of Saud Arabia with America, and "…the insufficiently harsh treatment reserved for Saudi Shiites."[117] In keeping with his Wahabbi tribal background, Juyayman believed that Shiites should be forced to accept Sunni Islam or face death. If there was a connection between the Iranian revolution and Juyayman's siege of the Grand Mosque, it would not be the inspiration of the Islamic revolution in a Shiite Iran. For Juyayman and his followers the Iranian revolution was more proof of Saudi Arabian weakness that they attributed to the Al-Saud's movement away from the traditions of the prophet Mohammed and his first three generations of followers.

Another source of influence for Juyayman and his followers was the Egyptian Muslim Brotherhood that the Al-Saud monarchy had allowed into the country. According to the author

---

[113] Pollack, 153.

[114] Trofimov, 2.

[115] Ibid., 68.

[116] Ibid., 33.

[117] Ibid., 32.

Trofimov, "Egyptian radicals were in total agreement with Juhayman that the current rulers of the Arab world—be it the Egyptian president or the Saudi king—were no longer legitimate because of their failure to defend the true faith and to stand up to the West."[118] Ayman Zawahiri, a member of the Egyptian Muslim Brotherhood in 1979 who would later become Osama Bin Laden's infamous right hand man, admired Juhayman's writings on the subject of Islam and the failure of the Saudi royal family. Juhayman's Wahhabi upbringing and pious beliefs had become fused with the more radical Salafi practice of takfir that allows for the killing of Muslims found being apostates.[119] It was Sayyid Qutb, the author of *Milestones* who "…fused together the core elements of modern Islamism: the Kharijites takfir, ibn Taymiyya's fatwas and policy prescriptions, Rashid Rida's salafism, Maududi's concept of the contemporary jahiliyya and Hassan al-Banna's (founder of the Muslim Brotherhood) political activism."[120]

The fight for the Grand Mosque lasted two weeks, required the Saudis to employ thousands of National Guard and Regular Army troops, and ended in hundreds of deaths. The Saudis even employed the assistance of French Commandos to help them expel the last of the extremists from the basement of the Grand Mosque.[121] The Saudis drove Armored Personnel Carriers inside the Mosque, fired artillery, and used chemical agents, all inside Islam's most holy. This use of weapons at the Grand Mosque, forbidden by the Koran, would later inspire other extremists.

During this two-week scare, the Kingdom also experienced an uprising by the Shiite minority in the eastern part of the country. This community occupied rich oil fields along the Persian Gulf. The already overstretched Saudi security forces were not even aware of the threat

---

[118] Ibid., 44.

[119] Ibid., 43.

[120] Benjamin and Simon, 62.

[121] Zuhur, 22.

and the king received his intelligence from the American Central Intelligence Agency.[122] Shiites inspired by the ongoing revolution in Iran, the events at the Grand Mosque, and the annual Ashura commemorating the martyrdom of Hussain, began an assault on Saudi security forces.[123] Trofimov stated, "[t]he weakness that Saudi forces displayed in the Grand Mosque emboldened these radicals to act in their own hometowns, opening a second front of the war against the hated regime."[124] The Saudi regime attempted to suppress the event just as it had done with the Grand Mosque affair. The Saudis blockaded the region and waited for the fervor to subside. The Saudi forces fought back when pressed, as collateral damage was not as great a concern when dealing with Shiites as it was in the Grand Mosque.

The Al-Saud regime had employed all of its resources to end the Grand Mosque episode. They attempted to contain that traumatic event as much as possible, however, word of the attack as well as the Shiite uprising did reach the outside world. During the episodes, the Saudis learned of the weaknesses of their security and intelligence forces to handle domestic threats and quickly concluded that external threats such as Iran were beyond their capability to confront. The reign of Ibn Abdel-aziz and his family had come precariously close to the brink of collapse and without foreign intervention from the French and support from the Americans would have likely ended.

For the Al-Saud regime, survival of the royal family once again became the primary focus of the government. Due to the growing Shiite threat, the breaking apart of the Sunni Arab cooperation that had dominated the region since the foundation of Israel, and the domestic scare at the Grand Mosque, King Fahd reached out to the United States to meet his family's security needs. Saudi security forces were incompetent and a possible threat to the family. Juyayman and many of his followers had served in the National Guard, a force that was supposed to protect the

---

[122] Trofimov, 180.

[123] Ibid.

[124] Ibid., 181.

royal family and its interest from the regular Army and Air Force.[125] The Al-Saud family sought

refuge in its strategic partnership with the west. The royal family was willing to act on the behalf

of the west by increasing oil production to keep crude prices low. For the United States, this

ended the oil crises that had plagued the country during the 1970s. For the future leader of Al-

Qaida, Osama Bin Laden, this would be the root of his discontent with the Saudi regime. The

Saudis used the USSR invasion of Afghanistan just two weeks after the end of the Grand Mosque

episode as a way to export the Kingdom's Islamic extremists. Bin Laden was one of the

volunteers. Later, in 1990 when Saddam Hussein's Iraq threatened the homeland of Bin Laden,

the King would choose help from the Americans over his Wahabbi warriors sent abroad to

Afghanistan to fight for Islam.[126]

Impact of 1979 on today: Al-Qaida

By the end of the Grand Mosque episode, the Al-Saud regime clearly recognized the

threat of Sunni Islamic extremism to the future of the kingdom. On December 25, 1979, the

Soviets invaded Afghanistan.[127] The Saudi government had been funding an Islamic insurgency

against the Communist government in Kabul. With the fall of Afghanistan to the Soviets, the

House of Saud now envisioned yet another threat to the future of the Al-Saud Kingdom.

The United States viewed the Soviet invasion of Afghanistan through the lens of the Cold

War. The Soviets were now one step closer to a deep water port on the Indian Ocean and capable

of striking American interests in the Persian Gulf.[128] The United States and Saudi Arabia shared

a stake in seeing the USSR defeated in Afghanistan. For the United States, this was an

opportunity not only to attack its Cold War opponent, the USSR, but also to support its Sunni

---

[125] Ibid., 25.

[126] Ibid., 247.

[127] Ibid., 235.

[128] Ibid,. 236.

ally, Saudi Arabia in the Islamic world. A desired side effect of the Afghanistan campaign was to draw Muslim attention away from Iran and redirect it toward the Saudi regime.

For Saudi Arabia, the Afghanistan front was not only a way to re-establish the Saudi domain over Islam and push back against the growing Shiite threat in Iran, but also an opportunity to export the Sunni extremist movement in the country. Yaroslav Trofimov writes, "[i]n 1980, the gates of jihad were opened. With a fatwa by Bin Baz (leader of the Saudi clerics) proclaiming jihad in Afghanistan an individual duty of every Muslim, mosques and universities across Saudi Arabia turned into recruitment centers for Islamic volunteers."[129] Osama Bin Laden, who was still loyal to the Saudi regime at the time of the call to jihad, was one of the first volunteers. Bin Laden left for Pakistan within a month of the Soviet invasion.[130] During his first trip to Afghanistan, Osama Bin Laden "…fell under the influence of the Jordanian Palestinian, Sheikh Dr. Abdullah Azzam" who was a "…stalwart of the Jordanian Muslim Brotherhood."[131] Abdullah Azzam and his protégé Osama Bin Laden worked together in the Afghanistan Services Bureau in Peshawar, Pakistan for many years.[132] Azzam founded Al-Qaeda in 1987 as an umbrella organization to bring the various Islamic factions and movements together and to provide a purpose and direction. Azzam envisioned Al-Qaeda as an international Islamic organization capable of providing and directing resources to various Islamic movements throughout the world. Osama Bin Laden assumed full control of Al-Qaeda after orchestrating the death of his mentor and ideological founder of Al-Qaeda in 1989.[133]

---

[129] Ibid., 244.

[130] Rohan Gunaratna, *Inside Al Qaeda: Global Network Of Terror* (New York: Berkley Book, 2002), 23.

[131] Ibid., 24.

[132] Ibid., 5.

[133] Ibid., 31.

Bin Laden and his newly acquired Al-Qaeda network were star pupils of the reborn Saudi Arabian Sunni sphere of influence throughout the 1980s. During this decade, the Pakistan, U.S., and Saudi Arabian alliance to defeat the USSR in Afghanistan was successful, and Saudi Arabia began to gain some ground in its regional struggle for power with its Shiite nemesis, Iran. However, unlike Iran who was able to control its 1979 proxy Hezbollah, Saudi Arabia would lose control of their 1979 offspring, Al-Qaeda. When in 1990 Saudi Arabia was threatened by the Iraqi invasion of Kuwait, the Al-Saud family called upon the United States during its hour of need and not Bin Laden. After the 1990-1991 Gulf War, Saudi Arabia became the target of Al-Qaeda, an organization led by a man who had been inspired by Juhayman and his seizure of the Grand Mosque. According to Trofimov, in 2004 Bin Laden commented that "…[Crown Prince] Fahd defiled the sanctity of the Grand Mosque."[134] It has been documented that Bin Laden stated in reference to Juhayman and his followers, "…the men who seized Mecca were true Muslims innocent of any crime."[135] For Saudi Arabia and the House of Saud, 1979 is the year of crisis and misguided decisions resulting in the regime creating its own greatest threat to survival, Al-Qaeda. Rohan Gunaratna writes that Osama Bin Laden

"sports a ring containing a black stone set in silver. From a strictly Islamic point of view, the stone symbolizes the Ka'aba, which in turn is the symbol of Mecca, the most revered holy place of Islam. This reminds us the viewer that Osama's principal goal is to free Mecca and the Arabian Peninsula both from foreign unbelievers (America and its allies) and the house of Al-Saud."[136]

---

[134] Trofimov, 246.

[135] Ibid., 247.

[136] Gunaratna, 56.

Afghanistan and 1979; The Opening of the Western Front in the War for Islam

The Great Game's new map

The great game between Russia and the British over central Asia used Afghanistan as the chessboard. The Russian desire was to extend their sphere of influence over central Asia and establish a deepwater port on the Indian Ocean. The British desire was to put as much space as possible between their colonial empire in India and the Russians. As part of this game, in 1893 the British established a border between Afghanistan and British India (modern day Pakistan) known as the Durand Line.[137] The purpose of this line was to prevent Russia from having a border with British India as well as a way for the British to attempt to break up the Pashtun tribes in the Waziristan region.[138]

World War I ended the Great Game as Russia became embroiled in the Bolshevik revolution and Great Britain found her forces overextended trying to quell the independence movement springing up all across the Middle East and British Indian Empire. On 8 August 1919, the British signed the Treaty of Rawalpindi that "…conceded the complete independence of Afghanistan, and relinquished control over Afghanistan's foreign relations."[139] Based on this treaty, the modern day Afghanistan was born. Immediately following its independence, Afghanistan entered into a treaty with the Bolsheviks that allowed the Russians to establish consulates throughout the new state of Afghanistan.

---

[137] Nicholas Schmidle, *To Live Or To Perish Forever: Two Tumultuous Years In Pakistan* (New York: Henry Holt and Company, 2009), 45.

[138] Tanner, 218.

[139] Fromkin, 422.

The USSR continued to be influential in Afghanistan providing over one billion dollars in military aid and one and a quarter billion dollars in economic aid by 1979.[140] The rise of a communist regime in Kabul began after the murder of Mohammed Daoud, the Afghanistan prime minister. The Marxists political party of the Democratic Republic of Afghanistan killed Daoud and introduced an agenda for the country that essentially undercut six-hundred years of Pashtun rule. The Pashtun tribes immediately revolted against the communist regime and it became clear that Afghanistan was descending into chaos. Against the advice of the senior military leadership, the Soviets decided to intervene militarily in Afghanistan.[141] On December 25, 1979, The Red Army crossed the Amu Darya River from the USSR into Afghanistan. The Soviet plan was to dispose of Prime Minister Hafizullah Amin, who had become difficult for the Soviets to work with, and replace him with Babrak Karmal—someone they thought could bring the tribes under control.[142] The Soviet goal was to be out of Afghanistan within six months with Afghanistan stabilized and retained under Soviet influence.[143]

1979 Soviet invasion of Afghanistan

The Soviet invasion of Afghanistan was the fourth significant event in the region during 1979. Most if not all of the regional and international players with interests in the Middle East were astounded by the continuous roller-coaster of events in this watershed year. While the Shiites were having a revival with the return of the Ayatollah in February, the Sunni were officially recognizing their failure to destroy Israel with the signing of the Egypt-Israeli Peace Treaty in March. As the Shiite crescendo continued throughout the year, the Saudi dream of a

---

[140] Tanner, 226.

[141] Ibid., 233.

[142] Ibid., 236.

[143] Dr. Jacob Kipp, interview by author, Ft. Leavenworth, KS, May 1, 2009.

definitive recognition of their singular leadership role in the Islamic world ended with the attack upon the Grand Mosque in November.

In less than twelve months, the Sunni campaign for the Levant was over and the newly declared regional power of Iran immediately began to take on the U.S.—Israel nexus, turning their rhetoric into successes in the Lebanese theater by 1983. To keep pace with the Shiite surge in power, the Sunni needed new battlefields to spread their influence through the Islamic principles of Dahwa and Jihad. In the last month of 1979, the Soviet Union provided the Sunni an opportunity in Afghanistan. However, the Sunni would not go it alone—they would fight with a coalition who all had different interests and motivations for participating in the Afghan war. The members of the Saudi Arabian Sunni coalition included the United States, Pakistan through their intelligence service the ISI, The Muslim Brotherhood and their Pakistani offspring Jamaat-e-Islami, and finally the Afghan contingent of the Saudi Arabian coalition, the Pashtuns.[144] The different motivations of each of these participants explain how Afghanistan has evolved into the eastern theater of war in the conflict between Shiite and Sunni for control of Islam.

To understand the complexity of the Afghan war, it is important to analyze the conflict from the perspective of each of the key participants starting with the external actors, the United States and Saudi Arabia. The United States viewed the Soviet invasion of Afghanistan through the lens of the Cold War. The weakness of the initial response by the Carter administration allowed the Soviets to believe that the invasion would go un-opposed by the United States. However, with the arrival of President Regan in January 1981, the mood had changed and the United States provided a response that would defeat the Soviet forces.[145]

---

[144] Ahmed Rashid, *Taliban: Militant Islam, Oil & Fundamentalism in Central Asia* (New Haven: Yale University Press, 2001), 130.

[145] Lesch, 56.

For the Regan administration, the defeat of the Soviets and victory in the Cold War was the ultimate prize. To this extent, the U.S. macro level view espoused the belief that Sunnis were allies against the Iranian Shiites who had held U.S. hostages for 444 days in Iran. Under this philosophy, U.S. support and participation in Afghanistan was a win-win scenario. A victory in Afghanistan would harm the Soviets while bolstering the Sunni against the Shiite Iranians. The ghost of Vietnam still overshadowed the conscience of the American public and the Regan administration knew that physically deploying U.S. troops to Afghanistan to fight the Soviets was not a feasible option. However, Saudi Arabia had an available pool of Islamic extremists readily available for deployment to the front lines and after the catastrophe of the Grand Mosque attack, the monarchy was more than ready to facilitate their transfer out of the Kingdom. The United States found itself in a position to contribute to the fight through the supply of money, and even more importantly, weapons. The United States provided the Afghan Mujahedeen approximately five billion dollars in funds between 1980 and 1992, matched dollar for dollar by Saudi Arabia for a total of ten billion dollars to the Sunni Islamists fighters.[146] As Mujahedeen success against the Soviets grew, the United States increased its commitment to the fight with three significant steps. The Central Intelligence Agency provided the Sunni jihadists with U.S. made Stinger missiles, U.S. trainers, and support to Pakistani ISI and Saudi Arabia in recruiting Islamists from around the region to make the trip to Pakistan for training and eventual fighting against the Soviets.[147]

The Saudi view of the Afghan war consisted of three critical areas related to self-interest of the al-Saud family and their continued concern for survival. The siege of the Grand Mosque had demonstrated the fragility of the kingdom. The Afghan campaign was an immediate opportunity for the Monarchy to demonstrate its leadership in the Islamic world and push back

---

[146] Rashid, 18.

[147] Ibid., 129.

against the Shiite tide. For example, on 26 December 1979, the day after the invasion of Afghanistan by the USSR, Osama Bin Laden left Saudi Arabia to assess the situation in Pakistan.[148] The Afghanistan campaign provided the opportunity for the royal family to transfer its growing internal extremist threat out of the borders of the Kingdom into Pakistan. With the transfer of the Islamists who had threatened the regime came the opportunity for Saudi Arabia to export its Wahabbi ideology and draw Afghanistan and Pakistan closer into the Saudi orbit.[149] Saudi Arabia could also promote Sunni Islam through the support of the Pashtuns who made up a majority of the Mujahedeen fighters. While Iran was heavily embroiled in a war with Saddam Hussein's Iraq during this same time, the Iranians did provide aid to the Shiite Hazaras in Afghanistan's central Hindu Kush region.[150] Saudi Arabia's vast oil wealth and access to the Pakistani Mujahedeen network established by the ISI and funded by the west gave Saudi Arabia a distinct advantage over the Iranians. Saudi Arabia also understood the connection between Pakistan and the Islamic regions farther to the east such as the Kashmir, Bangladesh, and the Muslim populations of Tajikistan, Uzbekistan, and Turkmenistan. An Islamic Jihadist training location in Pakistan with recruits from all over the Muslim world allowed Saudi Arabia to indoctrinate the Sunni Islamic world, increasing the penetration of Saudi Arabia's control over Islam and its position as regional power broker.

Lastly, Saudi Arabia was able to contribute to its greatest ally, the United States in its fight against the Soviets in the Cold War. While the Saudis and their confidants the Pakistanis, took on the leading role in the Afghanistan front, the U.S. was engaged in confronting the Iranians in Saudi Arabia's back yard, the Persian Gulf. This quid pro quo helped Saudi Arabia to keep America vested in a strategic alliance between the two nations. As the United States

---

[148] Gunaratna, 23.

[149] Rashid, 129.

[150] Tanner, 251.

destroyed Iranian naval vessels threatening Saudi oil shipments from the gulf, the Saudis

recruited, equipped, and funded a Sunni Army against the Soviets.[151]

For Pakistan, its geo-political situation in 1979 was dire. With India on the eastern border

threatening the survival of Pakistan, the nation on the eastern frontier of Islam could not afford a

communist nation on its western border isolating Pakistan from the Islamic world. In addition,

India - Pakistan's greatest concern - was an ally of the U.S. By helping the U.S. cause in

Afghanistan, Pakistan believed they could acquire leverage with the U.S. concerning the Kashmir

question. Much like Afghanistan, Pakistan was an amalgamation of various tribes and ethnicities

that really only shared Islam as an identity. For this reason, Islamism presented the Pakistani

leadership with an ideology that could unify the nation against internal and external threats.

According to Rashid, "President Zia aimed to cement Islamic unity, turn Pakistan into the leader

of the Muslim world and foster an Islamic opposition in Central Asia."[152] For these reasons, when

it came to supporting an Islamic movement in Pakistan and Afghanistan, the Pakistani position

was "all in."

For the Pashtuns, the fight against the Soviets was more than just pushing back

communism, it was also about returning the Pashtuns to power in Afghanistan. The Pashtun tribes

dominated the politics of Afghanistan over their regional minority counterparts for three hundred

years until Mohammed Daud Khan rose to power in 1973 with the help of the Soviet

Communists.[153] The Pashtun's insurrection against the Daud regime and his communist

supporters began almost immediately. Daud was helped to power by a small minority political

party whose motivation was to defeat a growing Islamic movement that by 1975 had spread all

across the Middle East and now into Afghanistan. After being chased out of Afghanistan by the

---

[151] Pollack, 231.

[152] Rashid, 129.

[153] Ibid., 21.

forces of Daud, "the leaders of this movement fled to Peshawar in 1975 and were backed by Pakistan's Prime Minister Zulfiqar Ali Bhutto to continue their opposition to Daud. These leaders, Gulbuddin Hikmetyar, Burhanauddin Rabbani and AhmadShah Masud were later to lead the Mujahidin."[154]

For the Americans, Saudis, and Pakistanis, this string of events turned out in their favor. An Islamic movement had come to Afghanistan just in time to support a Pashtun tribal conflict to regain control of Afghanistan from the Communist invaders. The result for the Sunni coalition was a Pashtun population ready and willing to fight the Soviet Army reinforced by Sunni extremists from across the Middle East. What none in the Sunni coalition expected, however, was that this Sunni Army would develop its own agenda for the Islamic world and eventually turn on the regimes that had sponsored them.

During the ten years of the Soviet—Afghan War, over 35,000 Islamists from forty-three different nations served in the Afghan Mujaheddin.[155] These radicals along with the Afghan freedom fighters brought the Soviets to their knees. These fighters were supported by U.S. and Saudi money and weapons, and they were trained by Pakistani ISI and American forces.[156] By 1986 the Soviets began a withdrawal from Afghanistan, and by 1989, the Soviets were gone. For the Soviets and the Americans the war was over. However, for the Sunni extremists imported to fight for Sunni Islam on the battlefields of Afghanistan, the war was now at home against their own governments and the west. For Saudi Arabia and Pakistan, the war had simply evolved into a new opportunity to continue to support the growing Deobandi movement, similar to the Saudi Arabian Wahabbi movement, on the eastern frontiers of the Islamic world. What remained in Afghanistan was a tremendous void.

---

[154] Ibid., 13.

[155] Ibid., 130.

[156] Ibid., 13.

The communist regime of President Najibullah managed to survive for three years before

being ousted from Kabul in 1992.[157] However, Kabul fell not to the Pashtuns, but to the Tajik and

Uzbek forces of Ahmad Shah Masud, Burhanuddin Rabbani and General Rashid Dostum.[158] The

Pashtun tribes refused subjugation by these ethnic minorities resulting in an Afghan civil war.

While various tribes, warlords, and extremists jockeyed for position in Afghanistan, the life of the

everyday Afghan citizen continued to get worse. Someone had to stand up for the Afghan people

who were continuing to suffer from the wars of the elites. These conditions created room for an

organization who declared that their aims were to "…restore peace, disarm the population,

enforce Sharia law and defend the integrity and Islamic character of Afghanistan."[159] The

majority of these individuals and groups were fed up with the fighting by 1994. They came from

the Madrasas that had been built by the ISI and funded by Saudi Arabia and the U.S. during the

Afghanistan - Soviet war from 1979 - 1989. These students organized themselves under the

leadership of Mullah Omar and called themselves the Taliban.

1979 in Afghanistan: The Roots of the Taliban

By 1989 the Soviet Union was defeated and had completed its withdrawal from

Afghanistan. The U.S. – USSR war on the soil of Afghanistan was over, but the war between

Saudi Arabia and Iran for control of the eastern frontier of the Islamic empire was heating up. The

reality of the Afghanistan—Soviet conflict was more complex than the defeat of one superpower

by another superpower and its Sunni allies. The U.S. and USSR let interest in Afghanistan

culminated in the ten years from 1979 to 1989. However, for the Sunni and the Shiite, 1979 was

the start of a grand design, both with the same end state. The 1979 movement to build the

---

[157] Ibid., 21.

[158] Ibid.

[159] Ibid., 22.

institutional infrastructure to supply Mujahedeen became the same apparatus that produced the Taliban. The Mujahedeen created a sphere of influence for Saudi Arabia on the eastern front and the evolution to the Taliban has allowed the house of Al-Saud to maintain its foothold. The Northern Alliance represents the Shiite effort to build an Army that would allow Iran its desired influence over Afghanistan. What once was old is new again. The old great game for control of central Asia had new players with new motives. Afghanistan is no loner the battleground for deep-water ports or buffer zones to protect trade routes. In this millennium it is the battleground for the eastern front in the Islamic Empire. For Sunnis, it is the gateway to Pakistan, Bangladesh, and the most populous Muslim nation in the world, Indonesia. For Iran, Afghanistan is a crucial buffer between them and thousands of Sunni extremists who view Shiites as worse than infidel westerners. With Iran focused on Israel, Lebanon, Syria, and Iraq to its west, Afghanistan represents the back door and Saudi Arabia's best chance to push back against its regional foe for control of Islam.

While 1979 is the beginning of the battle for the Islamic eastern frontier, 1989 represents the second campaign in this ongoing thirty year war. In 1989, the key players during the first decade of the war, the USSR and the United States pulled out, Iran, Saudi Arabia, and Pakistan emerge as the primary actors in the shaping of Afghanistan. For the Shiites, this effort would result in the building of its Shiite proxy Army in Afghanistan, the Northern Alliance.

The Iranian connection to the Northern Alliance is through the Shiite Hazara population, the largest Shiite group in a Sunni territory that resides in the central Hindu Kush region of Afghanistan.[160] The Iranians began to support their Shiite Afghani brothers with aid as early as 1980. After years of internal infighting between various Shiite factions within the Hazara population, the Iranian-backed Hazara Shiites joined the Northern Alliance in 1997.[161] The

---

[160] Ibid., 10.

[161] Tanner, 284.

Northern Alliance, a collection of Uzbeks, Tajiks, Turkmen, and Hazaras brought together by their common desire to defeat the Taliban, became a strategic partner for Iran who viewed the alliance as a way to prevent the emergence of a Sunni xenophobic neighbor on Iran's eastern border.

In 1998 the conflict between Iran and the Saudi Arabian proxy Taliban almost brought about an Iranian invasion of Afghanistan after the Taliban executed eleven Iranian diplomats and six thousand Hazaras in the city of Masar-i-Sharif.[162] The Iranians responded by deploying two hundred thousand republican guard soldiers to their border, however, the Iranians abandoned the effort for fear of entanglement in a protracted conflict on the eastern border of Iran when the main effort was in the Persian Gulf region.[163] The U.S. invasion in the winter of 2001 bolstered the Northern Alliance and many former leaders of the organization became members of the Hamid Karzai government with responsibilities such as interior, intelligence, and defense. With the help of the United States, Iran has achieved a significant foothold in the affairs of its Sunni dominated neighbor to the east.

While Iran has backed the anti-Taliban Northern Alliance, Pakistan and Saudi Arabia have backed the Taliban.[164] For decades the leader of Sunni Islamism, the Al-Saud Monarchy of Saudi Arabia spent billions of dollars and provided resources to spread Wahabbism across the Muslim world. Saudi Arabia has been particularly concerned with competing in areas where the Iranians were not, such as Europe and South East Asia. They have also confronted Iran in the traditional Middle East region through proxies such as Al-Qaeda. However, Saudi Arabia lost control of Al-Qaeda and its associated organizations when it chose the U.S. as its champion

---

[162] Ibid., 285.

[163] Pollack, 329.

[164] Rashid, 5.

against Saddam Hussein in the 1990-1991 Gulf War.[165] This rejection of Al-Qaeda and its leader Bin Laden placed the eastern frontier in jeopardy for the Saudis during the rise of the Taliban from 1994 to 1998. The old infrastructure that Saudi Arabia used to recruit, train, and equip the Mujahdeen during the Afghan Soviet campaign still exists in Pakistan and through this mechanism Saudi Arabia has been able to influence an intermediary between the Sunni leadership in Saudi Arabia and its breakaway proxy Army in Afghanistan. That intermediary is the Taliban.

Saudi Arabia first gained contact with the Taliban in the winter of 1994 by sponsoring hunting trips for Saudi royals to Afghanistan.[166] Through this first contact, Saudi Arabia grew to become a major sponsor of the Taliban and regain some ground against its Iranian competitor. As the Taliban grew, so did Saudi influence. In 1998, the Saudi-backed Taliban pushed the Iranian-backed Northern Alliance out of the last major city in the north. The two superpowers of Islam were now going toe to toe with each other through proxy armies, much like the actors of the great game of old.

After the attacks of September 11, 2001, and the subsequent invasion of Afghanistan that winter, Saudi Arabia conceded to accommodate its western ally, the United States. Saudi Arabia found itself stuck between wanting to support its western allies and not damaging its long efforts to exert its influence over the region. By providing only feeble support to the U.S. led efforts in Afghanistan, Saudi Arabia is prepared to reap the benefits of a growing Sunni Islamists movement that will give Saudi Arabia the upper hand in its struggle against Shiite Iran on the eastern front. During two years in Pakistan author Nicholas Schmidle found that the growing Islamist movement in Pakistan reflects the Sunni-Shiite conflict. Schmidle found jihadist groups,

---

[165] Gunaratna, 37-39.

[166] Rashid, 201.

such as Sipah-e-Sababa that "considered Americans, Canadians, and all other "crusaders" legitimate targets, but he saved most of his vitriol for Shi'ites."[167]

CONCLUSION

1979 was not the beginning of the Shiite-Sunni conflict - this conflict is as old as Islam itself. 1979, from the Levant to Kashmir, is a year of re-emergence. In emergence theory, the actions of one entity influence the other entities within a system.[168] In 1979 the paradigm in the Middle East changed dramatically with sudden emergence of a new entity, the Islamic Republic of Iran. For the Sunni Middle East, this was a game changer and could not have happened at a worse time. The emergent behavior of the 1979 influence is the growing Sunni - Shiite conflict for the control of Islam. In this instance, this emergent behavior does not bring order but instead delivers increased tension, competition, and chaos in the Islamic world.

The events of 1979 weaken Sunni domination in the Middle East, making room for a peer competitor: Iranian led Shiite Islam. The Iranian Islamic revolution was not a causal outcome of these events in the Sunni world, however, the diminution of Sunni leadership began in 1979 and continued over the next thirty years. This allowed for a more rapid expansion of Shiite power and prestige. The Soviet invasion of Afghanistan in 1979 served as a catalyst for the Sunni world to reorganize after the failures of Pan-Arabism and Secular Islam into a new Sunni construct. The new ideology for Sunnis from 1979 onward has been characterized by Islamic extremism in the form of Wahhabi, Deobandi, and Salafi ideological convergence in Afghanistan against a common enemy, the West. With victory over the USSR and the sharp decline in U.S. interests in Afghanistan and Pakistan, Saudi Arabia exploited the existing infrastructure that had produced

---

[167] Schmidle, 16.

[168] Steven Johnson, *Emergence* (New York: Scribner, 2001), 88.

the Mujahedeen to create their own Islamic Army to achieve their political goal of regional hegemony.

As the Sunni fundamentalist movement realized its efforts along the eastern front of the historic Islamic empire, the Shiites expanded in the west. The Shiites capitalized upon the fervor of the revolution and the rhetoric of Ayatollah Khomeini and exploited the Sunni failures against Israel on the western front. Iran infiltrated Lebanon, absorbed the insurgent movement and achieved one success after another beginning with withdrawal of U.S. troops from Beirut, Lebanon in February 1984, and the withdrawal of Israel from Lebanon in October 2000. [169] This victory combined with Iran's victory through its proxy Hezbollah in the summer of 2006 over Israel continues 1979's emergent trend of a growing Shiite power. This Shiite power has become so attractive on the western front that Sunni organizations such as Hamas have fallen under the spell of the Iranian regime, moving away from what they perceive as weak and leaderless Sunni organizations like the Egyptian Muslim Brotherhood and moving towards Iran. [170]

The Sunnis, likewise, defeated a superpower when the USSR withdrew from Afghanistan in 1989. However, while the Iranians were staying true to the principles of the 1979 revolution, Saudi Arabia called upon the U.S. to defend it from Saddam Hussein in 1990 and allowed the U.S. to maintain a presence in the region. For this, Saudi Arabia lost control of the Sunni movement that had achieved victory on the battlefield of Afghanistan, bringing about a new actor in the Islamic world, Al-Qaeda.

Saudi Arabia finds itself pulled between its Western allies pushing for Saudi support in the Global War on Terrorism and the Sunni Islamic movement that broadcasts every Saudi capitulation to the west as another sign of Saudi support to the infidels. The Sunni fundamentalists also claim that the Al-Saud families close ties with the west makes the royals

---

[169] Pollack, 205.

[170] Levitt, 26.

kefirs, an Islamic term in which a practicing Muslim is found un-Islamic and is perceived culturally to be worse than an infidel. Saudi Arabia today finds itself alone, threatened externally by Iran and internally by the Sunni extremist organizations that it helped to create. For these reasons, Saudi Arabia needs the growing Sunni Islamic movement that has emerged on the eastern frontier following the 1979 invasion of Afghanistan. The Taliban and its associated organizations, such as Lashkar-e-Tiba - responsible for the December 2008 Mumbai, India attacks - are the future of Sunni Islam if the Sunnis are to prevent the continued spread of Iranian domination. While these organizations pose a threat to Saudi Arabia, they pose an even greater threat to Iran. Thirty years of Saudi financial support toward building Madrasas that preach Wahhabism and sparked a homegrown frontier revival of extremist ideology has created a ground swell of anti-Shiite sentiment. The irony of the Sunni Islamic movement, according to a leader in the Pakistani Taliban interviewed by Nicholas Schmidle in 2007, is that "Pakistan will be like Iran was in 1979."[171]

Egypt has continued on its path towards a western model since its historic treaty with Israel in 1979. With Iraq and Syria under the control of the Iranians and Egypt and Jordan occupying positions of relative neutrality, the western front has all but been conceded to Iran, thus creating a situation that was unthinkable prior to 1979: Sunni interest in a stable and strong Israel. As recently as July 2009, reports have surfaced alleging Saudi Arabian tacit agreement to allow Israeli strike aircraft to use Saudi Arabian airspace in an attack against suspected Iranian nuclear research and development facilities.[172] The recent violence in Iraq has been at the national level along sectarian lines between Shiite and Sunni. The growing Sunni extremist movement on the eastern front is radically anti-Shiite. What these current atmospherics point to is

---

[171] Schmidle, 12.

[172] Mahnaimi, Uzi Mahnaimi and Sarah Baxter, "Saudis give nod to Israeli raid," *The Sunday Times*, July 5, 2009, under "Saudi support to Israel to attack Iran," http://www.timesonline.co.uk/tol/news/world/middle_east/article6638568.ece

that the macro-level geopolitical divide in the current Middle East is based on religious affiliation between Shiite and Sunni. These current tensions are rooted in the events of 1979.

The crisis in the Middle East is not about the west - it is about Islam and who gets to lead and control it. Islam has been a political force in the region since the time of Mohammed in 400 A.D. Over this sixteen hundred year history the influence of Islam has ebbed and flowed as the narrative of the Middle Eastern peoples has changed. The events of 1979 re-ignited Islamic history as the dominant political force, and hence the center of gravity for those seeking power. Any good politician needs an adversary. For the Sunni and Shiite power seekers, their best adversary is each other. Islam is everything: it is the government, the religion, the very fabric of society, a complete way of life. 1979 revitalized the power of Islam in Iran and thirty years of Shiite success has continued to amplify the strength of the Islamic movement. The Shiites have dominated the first thirty years of this conflict. However, the Sunnis are on the rise in the eastern front. Iraq and Afghanistan are on the borders of the Shiite Empire. There exists the potential for this war to move away from the periphery and into the heart of the Muslim world. Americans and their western allies must understand the significant of these two conflicts. It is not just the future of Iraq and Afghanistan that is at stake, but the future of the Islamic world.

BIBLIOGRAPHY

Afsar, Shahid, Chris Samples, and Thomas Wood. "The Taliban: An Organizational Analysis." *Military Review*, 2008: 58-73.

Baer, Robert. *The Devil We Know: Dealing with the New Iranian Superpower.* New York: Random House, 2008.

Benjamin, Daniel, and Steven Simon. *The Age Of Sacred Terror.* New York: Random House, 2002.

Black, Ian. "Fear of A Shia Full Moon." *Guardian.* January 26, 2007. http://www.guardian.co.uk (accessed July 12, 2009).

Chehabi, H.E., ed. *Distant Relations: Iran and Lebanon in the last 500 years.* Oxford: The Centre for Lebanese Studies, 2006.

Crocker, Ambassador Ryan. "Lessons of Diplomacy in the Middle East." Ft. Leavenworth, April 23, 2009.

Diker, Daniel. *Iran, Hizbullah, Hamas And the Global Jihad.* Jerusalem: Jerusalem Center for Public Affairs, 2007.

Fromkin, David. *A Peace To End All Peace: Creating The Modern Middle East 1914-1922.* New York: Henry Holt and Company, 1989.

Giustozzi, Antonio. *Koran, Kalashnikov, And Laptop: The Neo-Taliban Insurgency in Afghanistan.* New York: Columbia University Press, 2008.

Grau, Lester W., and Ali Ahmad Jalali. *The Other Side Of The Mountain: Mujahideen Tactics in the Soviet-Afghan War.* Leavenworth: Foreign Military Studies Office, 1995.

Gunaratna, Rohan. *Inside Al Qaeda: Global Network Of Terror.* New York: Berkley Book, 2002.

Harik, Judith P. *Hezbollah: The Changing Face of Terrorism.* New York : I.B. Tauris, 2007.

Hourani, Albert. *A History of the Arab Peoples.* New York: Warner Books Edition, 1991.

International Institute for Counter-Terrorism. "ICT's Jihad Websites Monitoring Group". 2008. http://www.ict.org.il/ (accessed September 12, 2009).

Israeli Intelligence Heritage & Commemoration Center. "The Intelligence and Terrorism Information Center". 2009. http://www.terrorism-info.org.il (accessed March 3, 2009).

Johnson, Steven. *Emergence.* New York: Scribner, 2001.

Khadduri, Majid. *War and Peace in the Law of Islam.* London: The John Hopkins Press, 1955.

Kinzer, Stephen. *All The Shah's Men: An American Coup and the Roots of Middle East Terror.* Hoboken: John Wiley & Sons, 2003.

Lesch, David W. *1979: The Year That Shaped the Modern Middle East.* Cambridge: Westview Press, 2001.

Levitt, Matthew. *HAMAS: Politics, Charity, and Terrorism in the Service of Jihad.* New Haven: Yale University Press, 2006.

Mahnaimi, Uzi, and Sarah Baxter. "Times Online." *timesonline.co.uk.* July 5, 2009. http://www.timesonline.co.uk/tol/news/world/middle_east/article6638568.ece (accessed August 27, 2009).

Malik, S.K. *The Quaranic Concept of War.* Delhi: Adam Publishers, 1992.

Pargeter, Alison. *The New Frontiers of Jihad: Radical Islam in Europe.* Philadelphia: University of Pennsylvania Press, 2008.

Paz, Reuven. *The Project for the Research of Islamists Movements.* 2002. http://www.e-prism.org (accessed March 3, 2009).

Peters, Gretchen. *Seeds Of Terror: How Heroin Is Bankrolling The Taliban and Al Qaeda.* New York: St. Martin's Press, 2009.

Pollack, Kenneth M. *The Persian Puzzle.* New York: Random House, 2004.

Rashid, Ahmed. *Taliban: Militant Islam, Oil & Fundamentalism in Central Asia.* New Haven: Yale University Press, 2001.

Roberts, Hugh. *The Battlefield Algeria 1988-2002: Studies in a Broken Polity.* New York: Verson Books, 2003.

Sachar, Howard M. *The Emergence of the Middle East: 1914-1924.* New York : Alfred A. Knopf, 1969.

Said, Edward W. *Orientalism.* New York: Random House Books, 1962.

Schanzer, Jonathan. *HAMAS Vs. FATAH: The Struggle For Palestine.* New York: Palgrave MacMillan, 2008.

Schmidle, Nicholas. *To Live Or To Perish Forever: Two Tumultuous Years In Pakistan.* New York: Henry Holt and Company, 2009.

Smith, B. C. *Understanding Third World Politics: Theories of Political Change & Development.* Bloomington: Indiana University Press, 1996.

Taheri, Amir. *Iran Press Service.* March 30, 2006. http://www.iran-press-service.com/ips/articles-2006/march-2006/iran_us_30306.shtml (accessed October 13, 2009).

Takeyh, Ray. *Hidden Iran: Paradox and Power in the Islamic Republic.* New York: Henry Holt and Company, 2006.

Tanner, Stephen. *Afghanistan.* Cambridge MA: Perseus Books Group, 2002.

The Electronic Intifada. 2009. http://electronicintifada.net/ (accessed October 12, 2009).

The Jerusalem Post. 2009. http://www.jpost.com (accessed July 8, 2009).

Trofimov, Yaroslav. *The Siege of Mecca: The 1979 uprising at Islam's Holiest Shrine.* New York: Random House, 2007.

Yapp, M.E. *The Making Of The Modern Near East 1792-1923.* New York: Longman Inc. , 1987.

Yapp, M.E. *The Near East Since the First World War.* New York: Longman Group , 1991.

Zuhur, Sherifa. *Saudi Arabia: Islamic Threat, Political Reform, and the Global War on Terror.* monograph, Carlisle: Strategic Studies Institute, 2005.